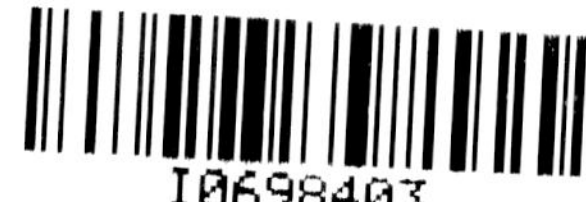

MY FLOWER COLORING BOOK

Volume I

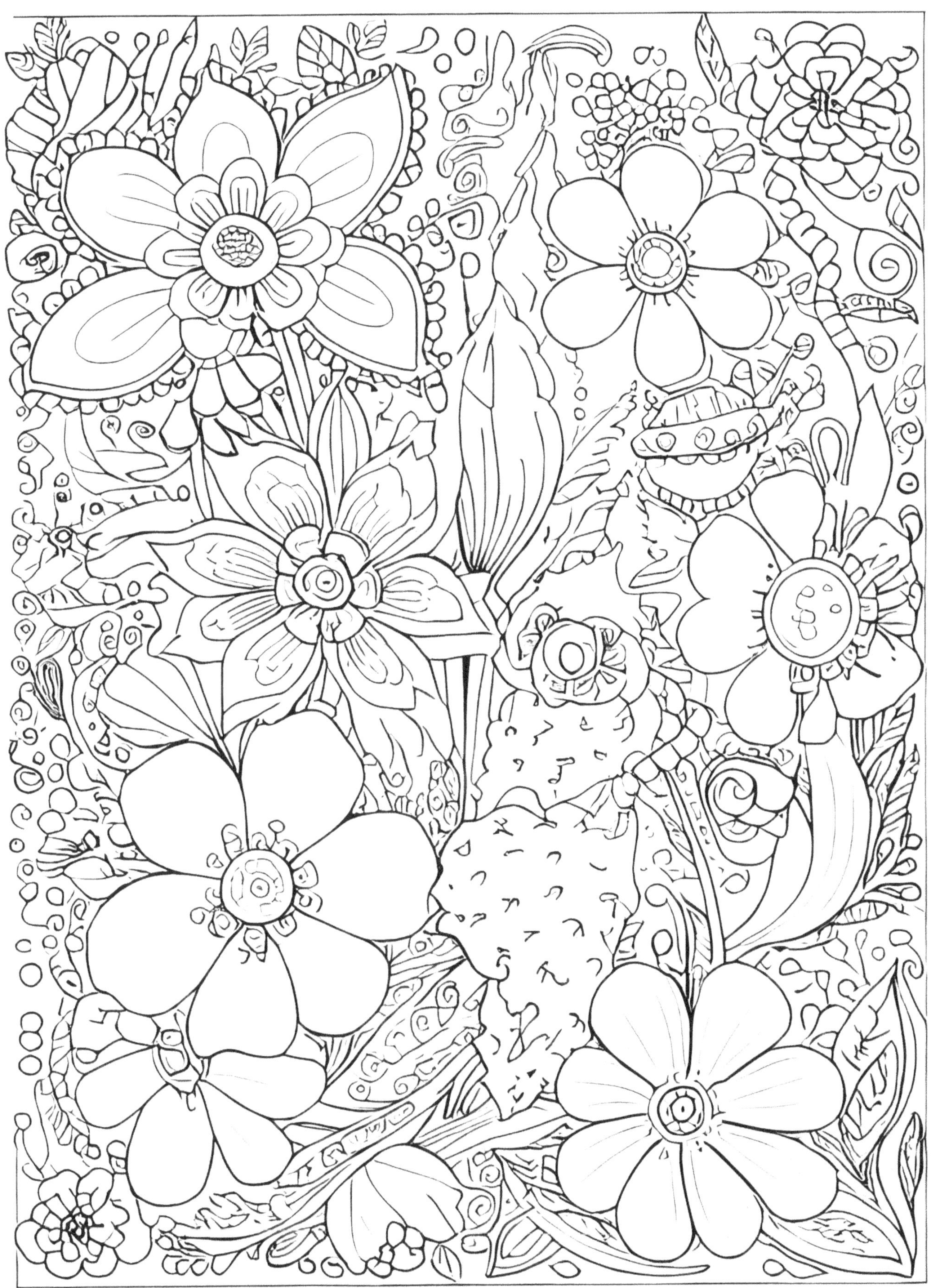

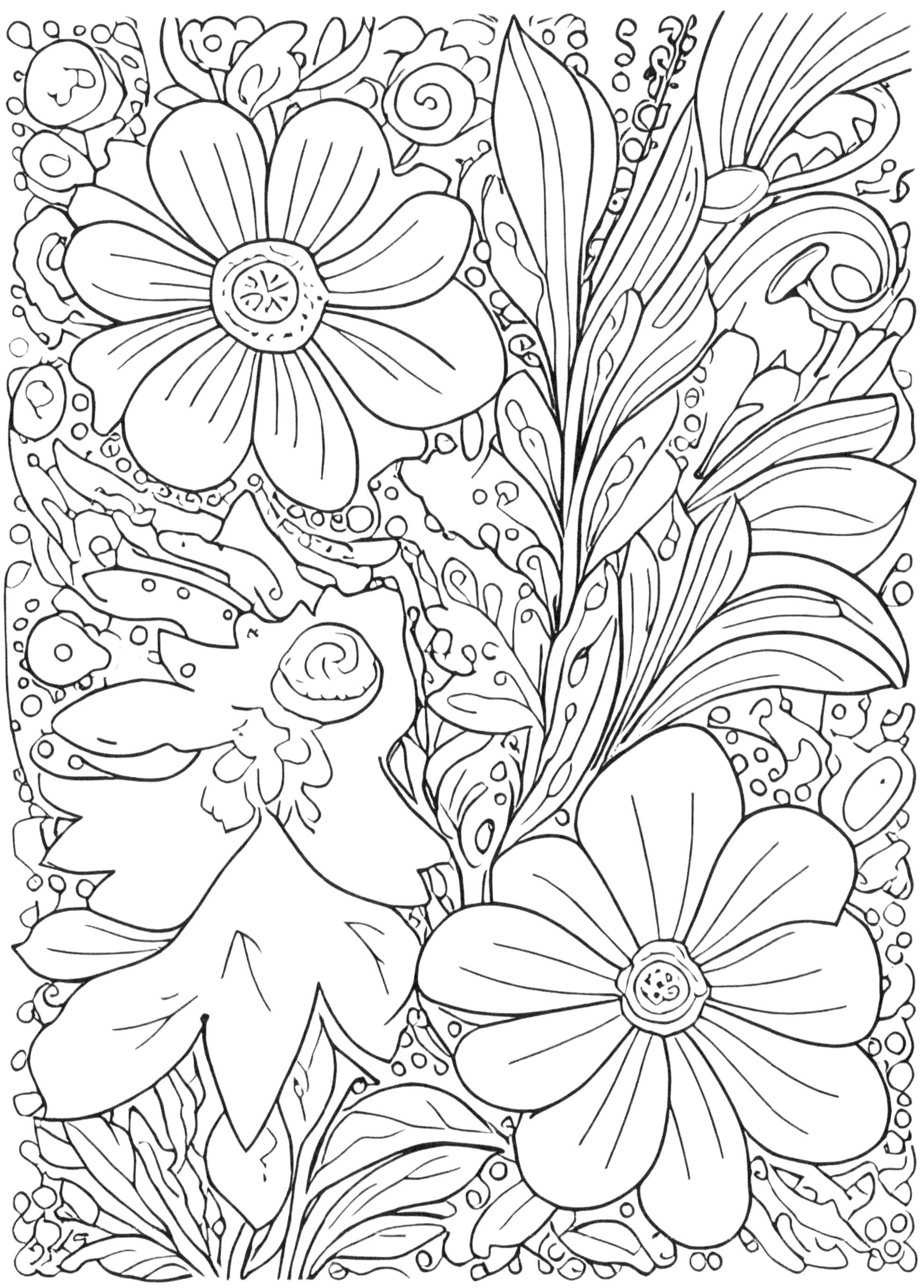

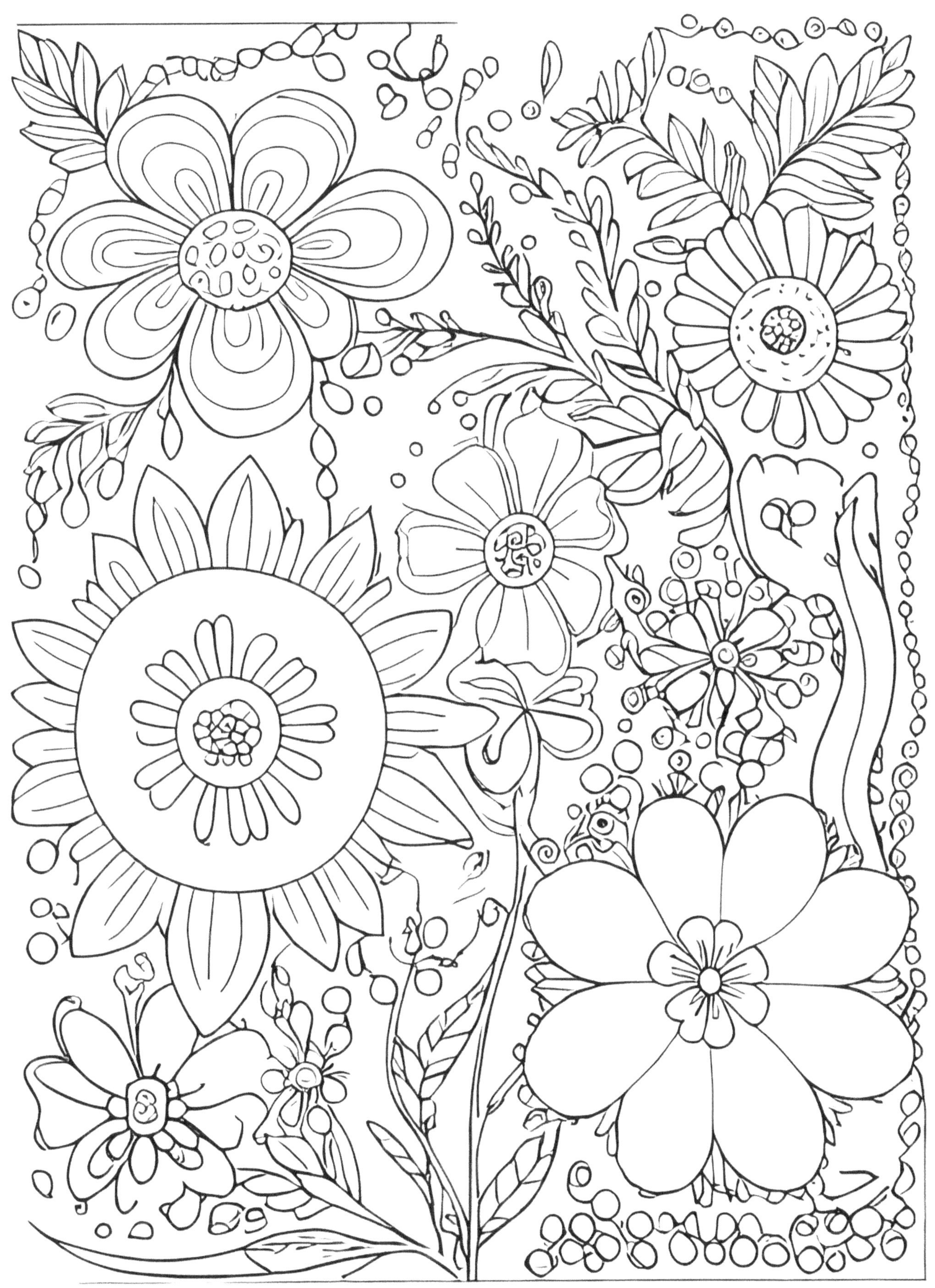

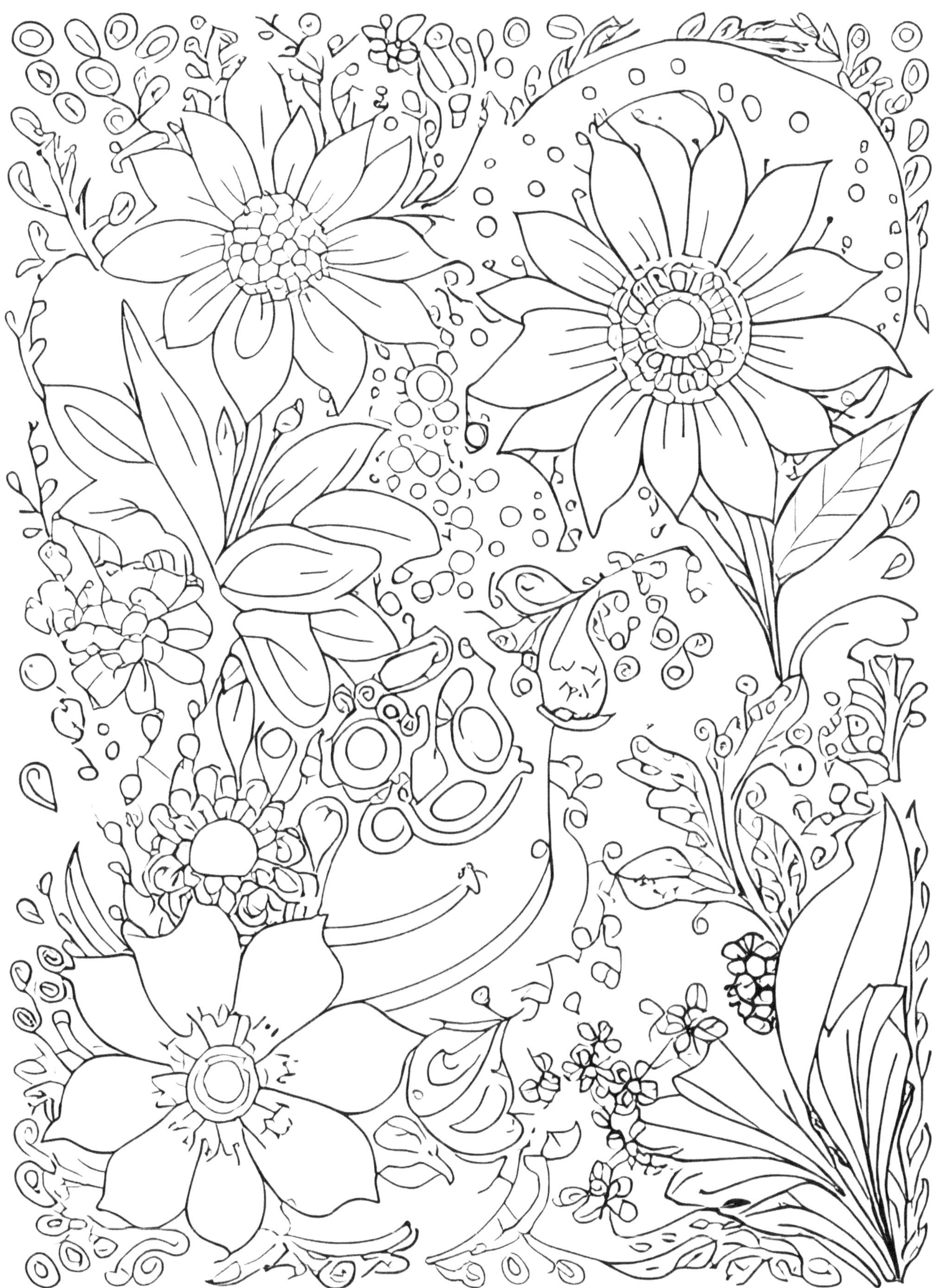

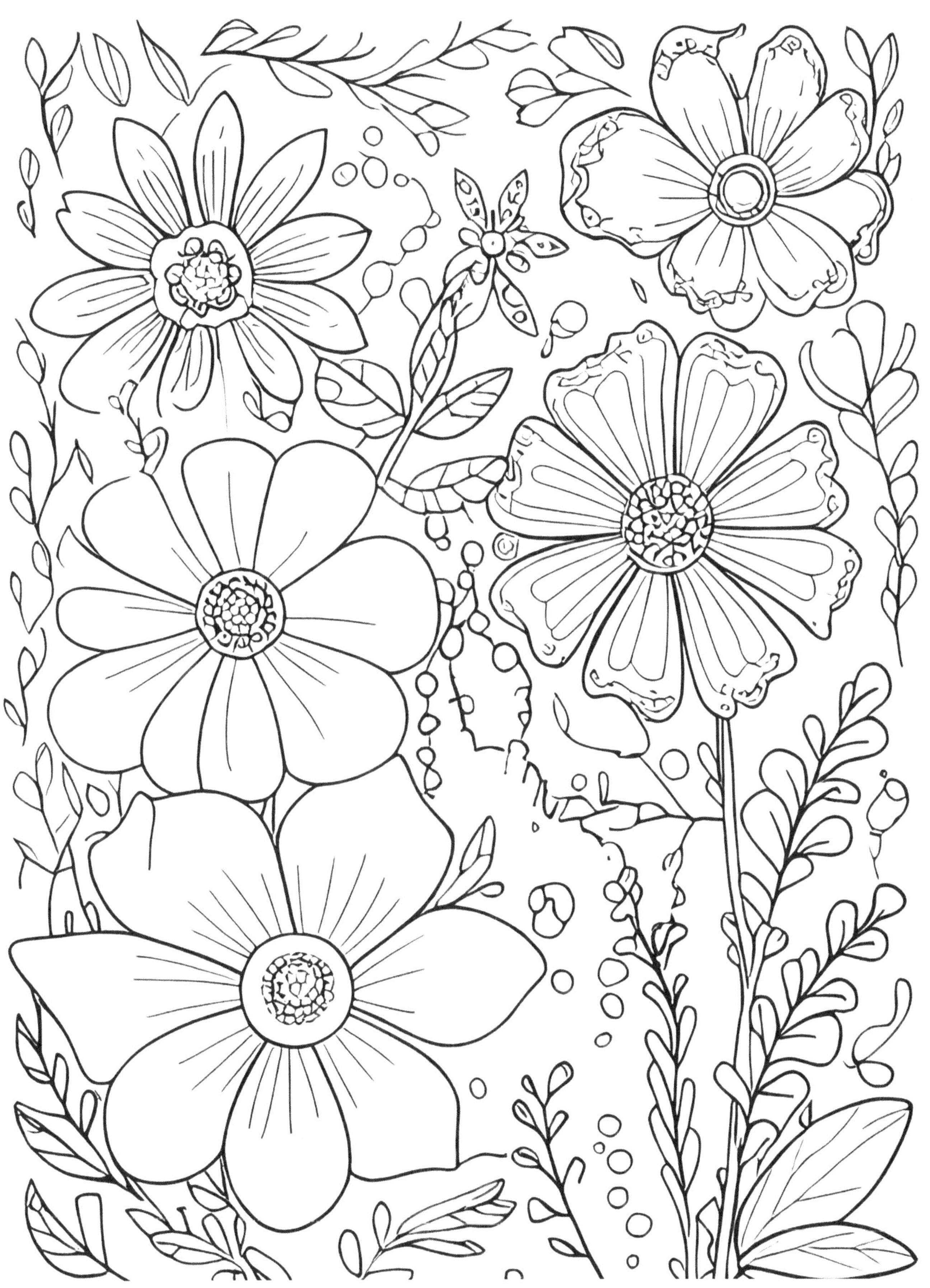

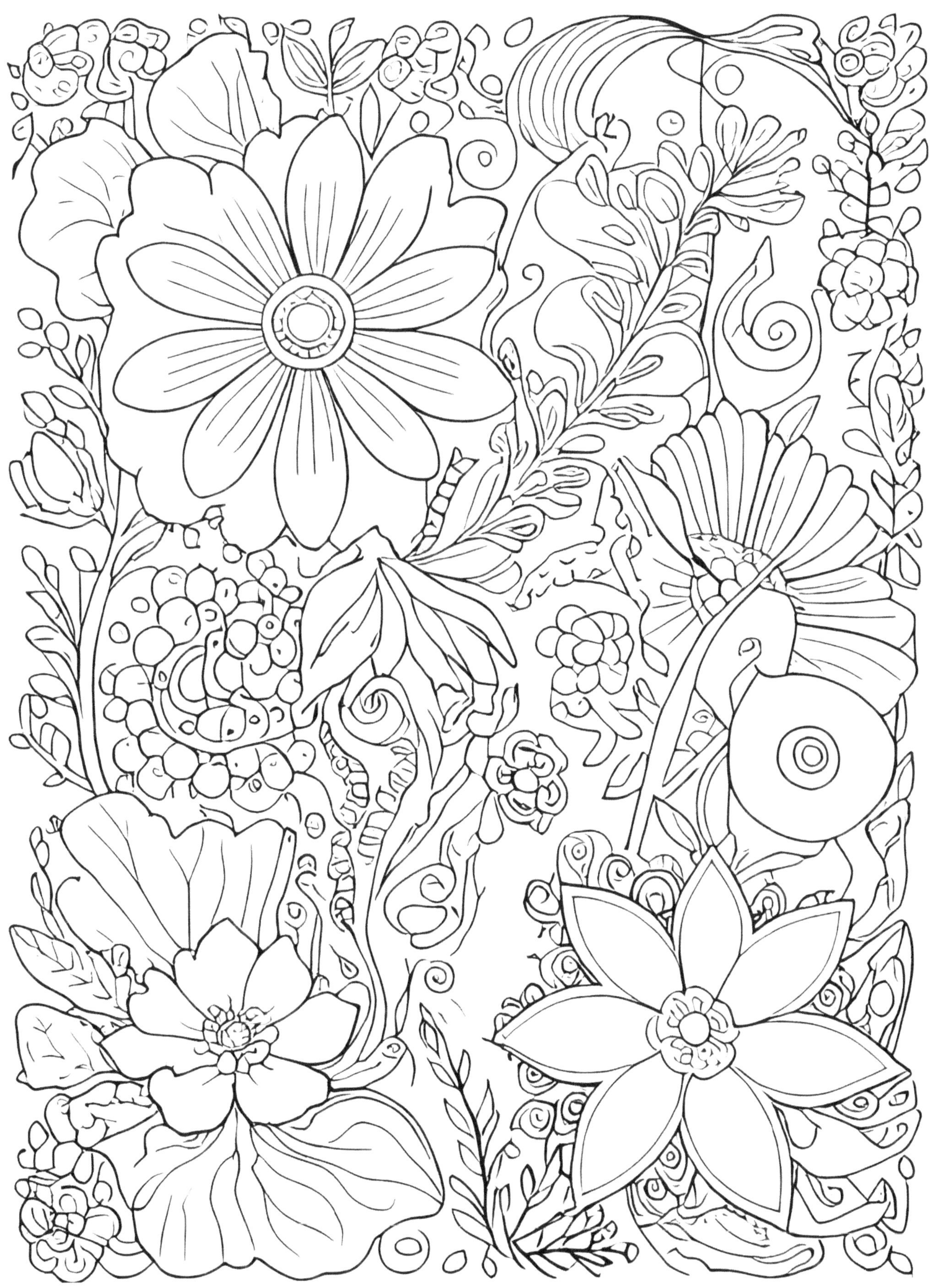

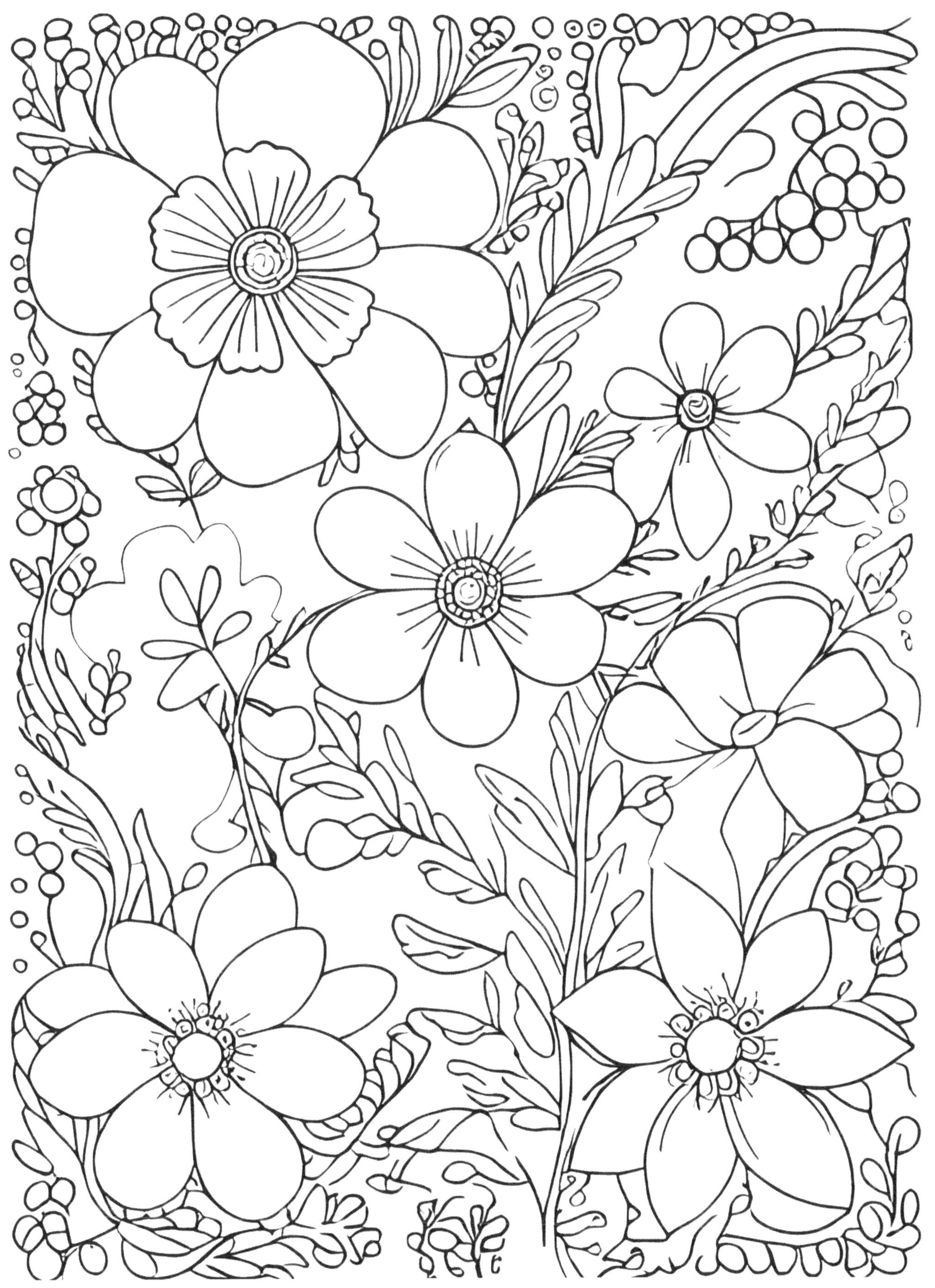

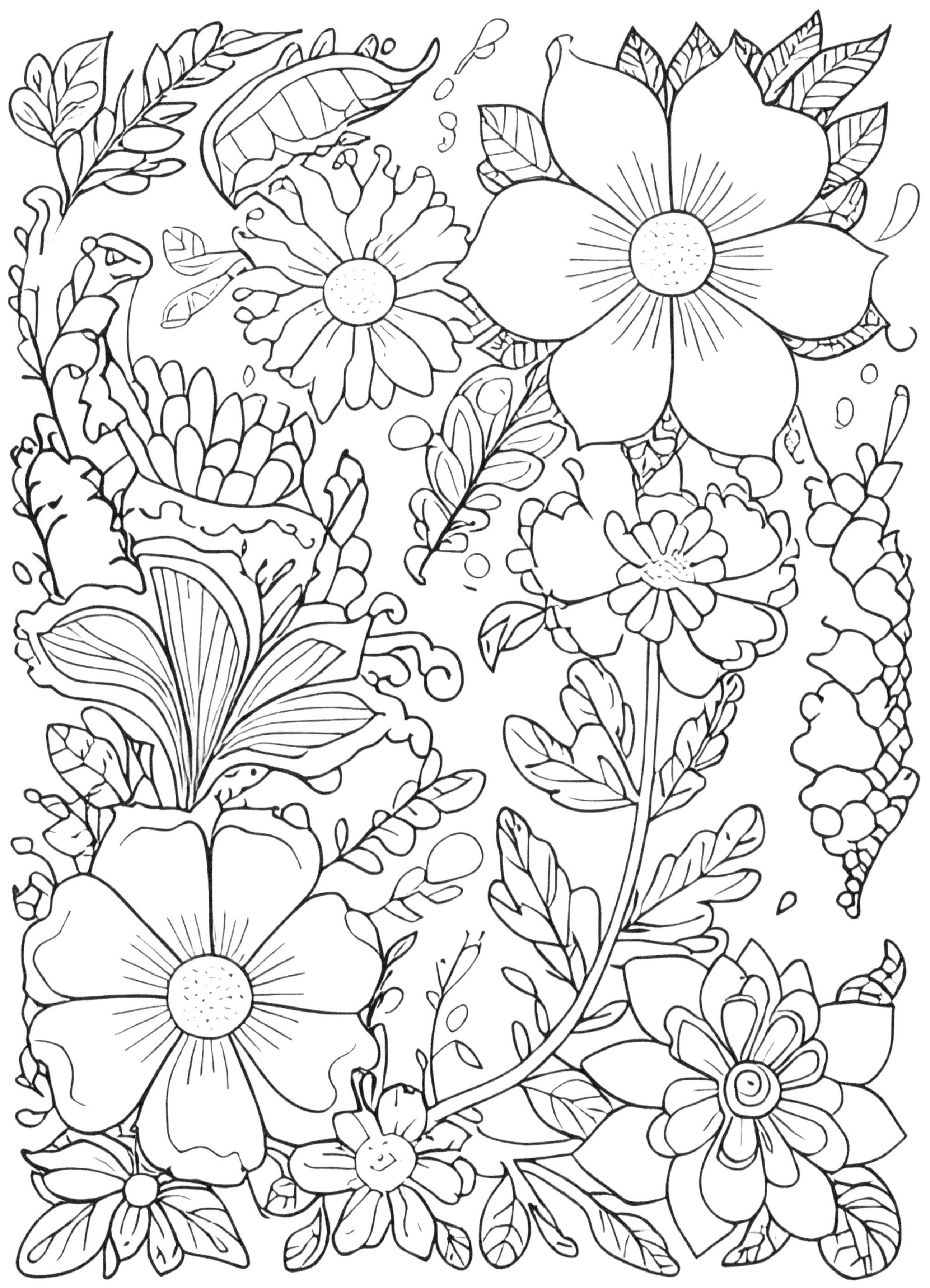

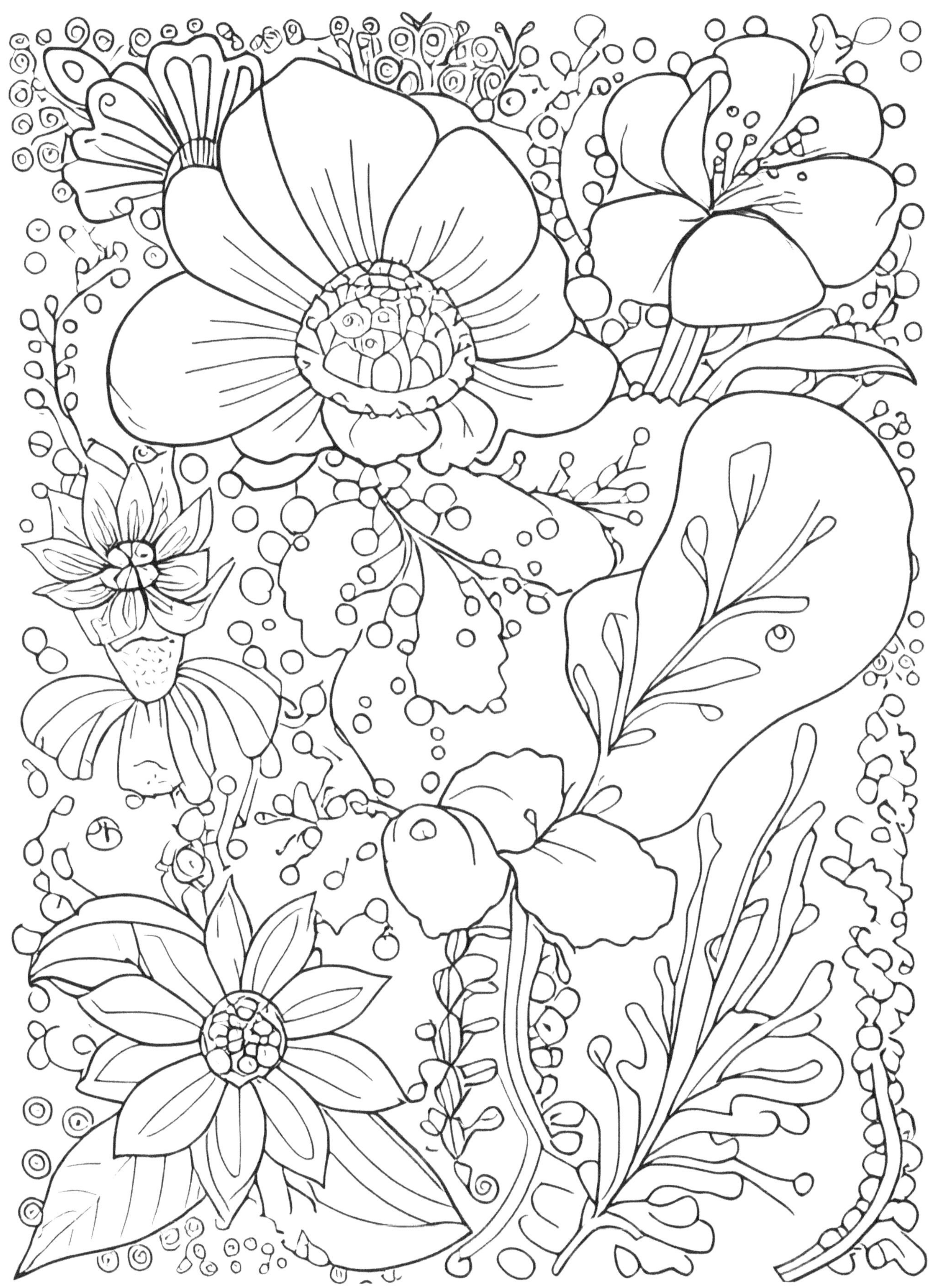

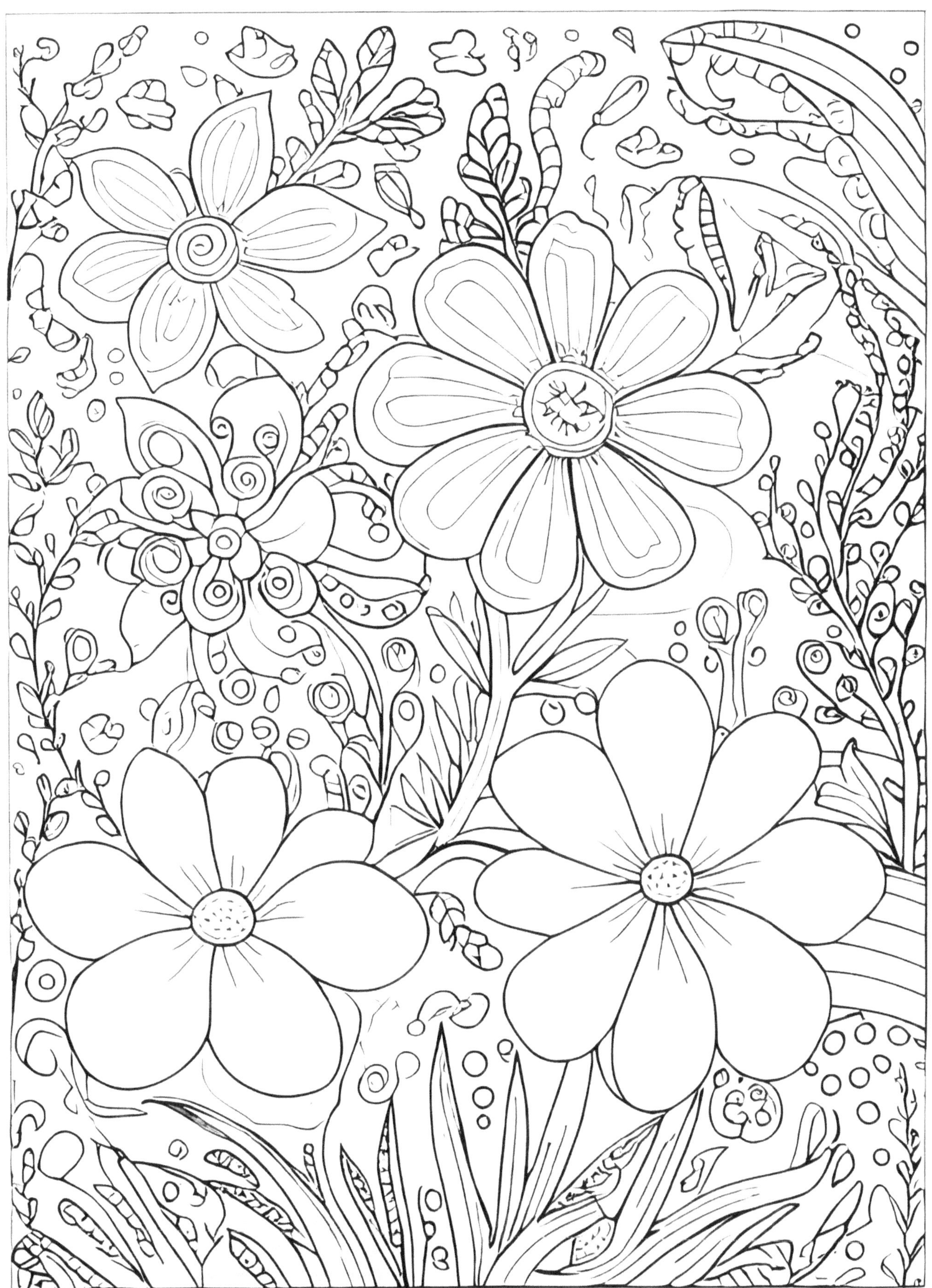

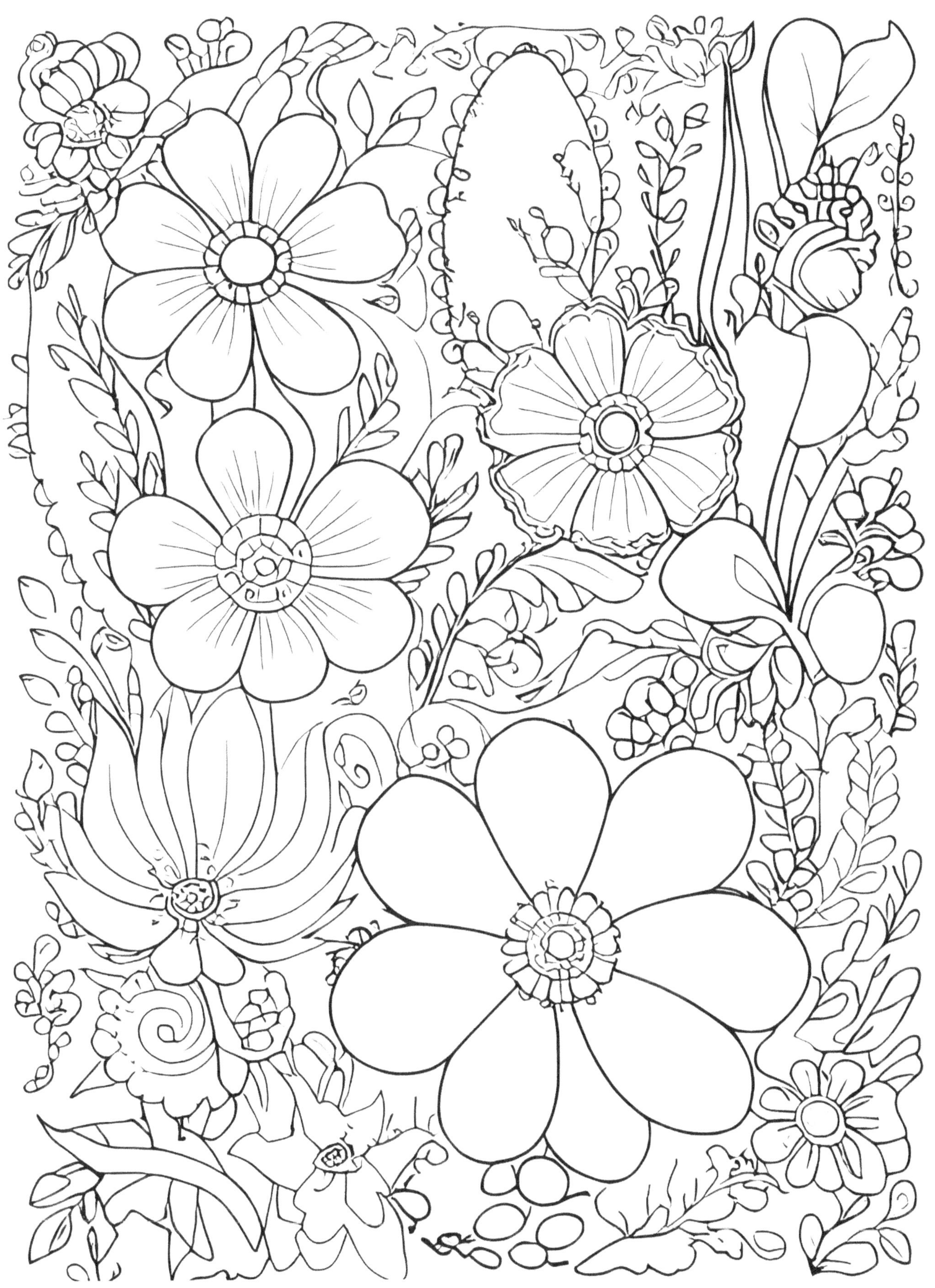

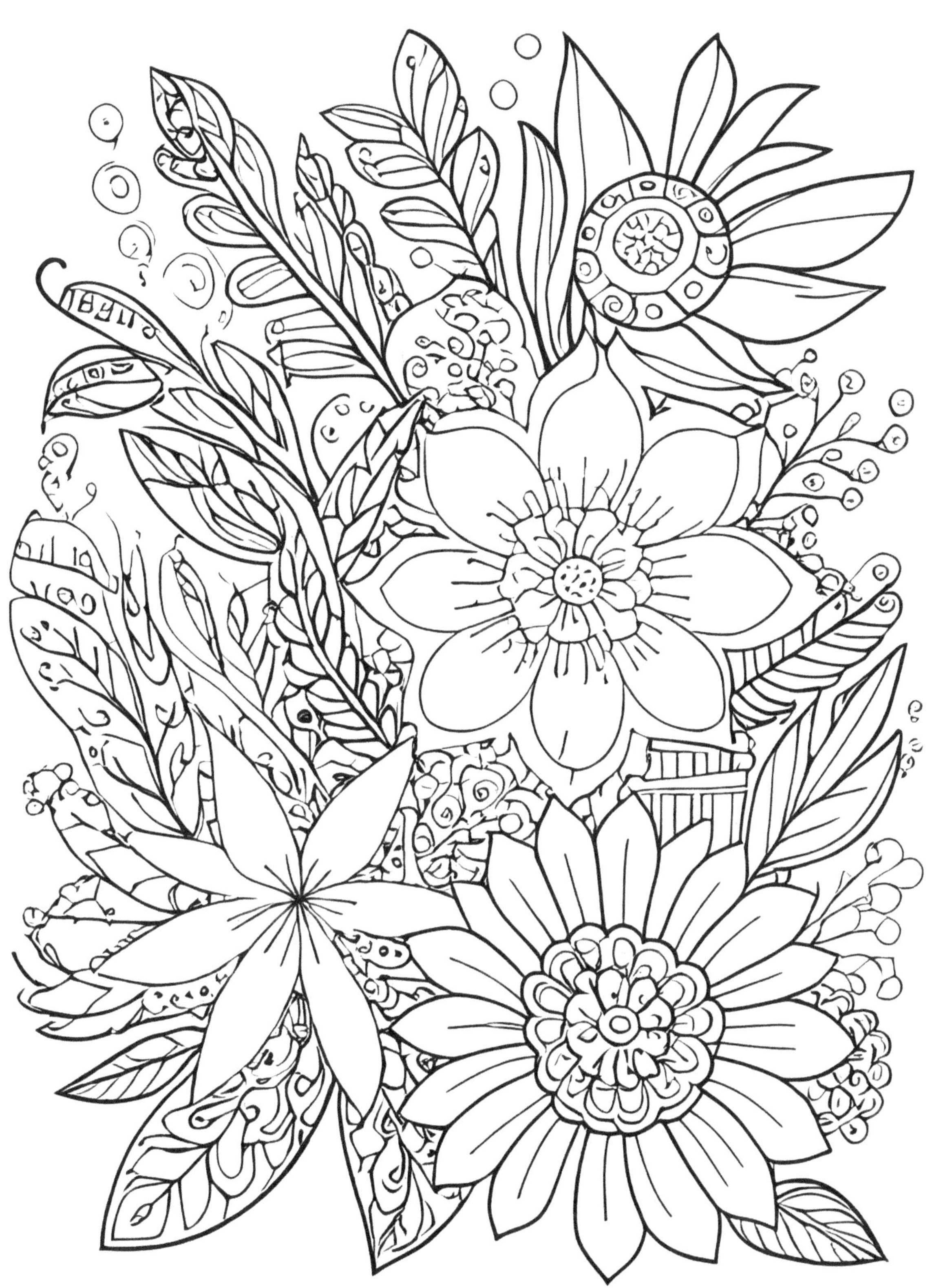

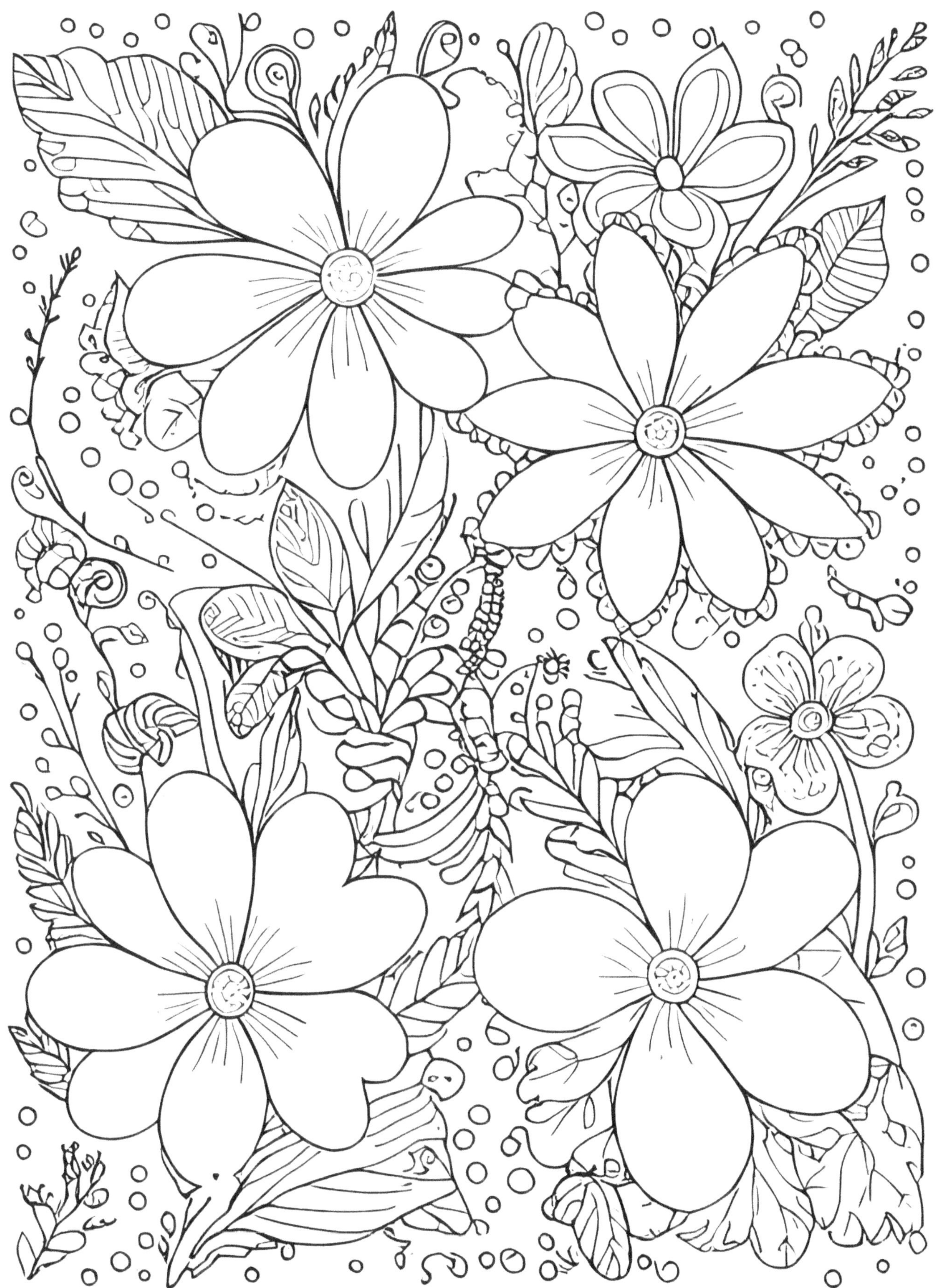

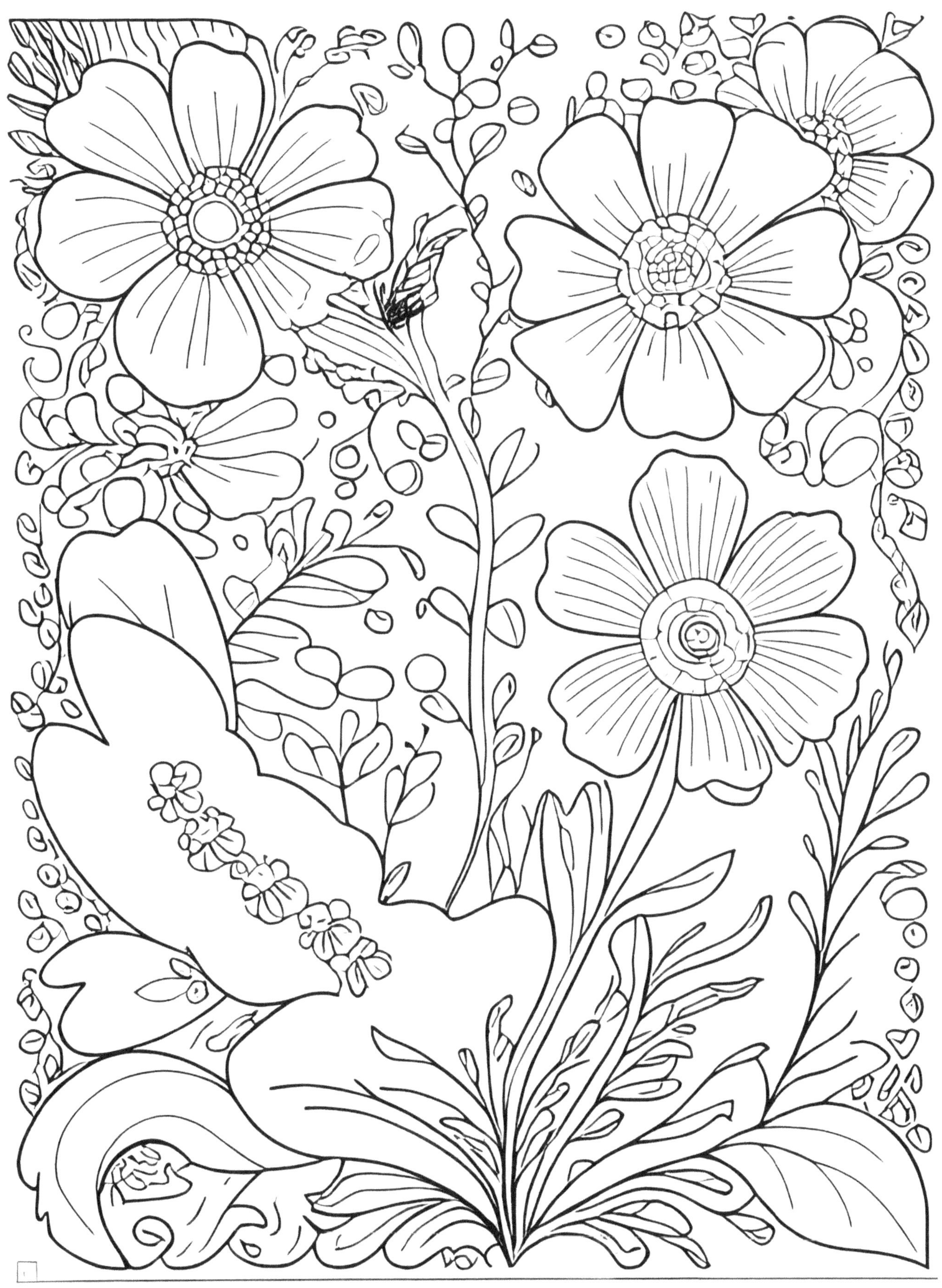

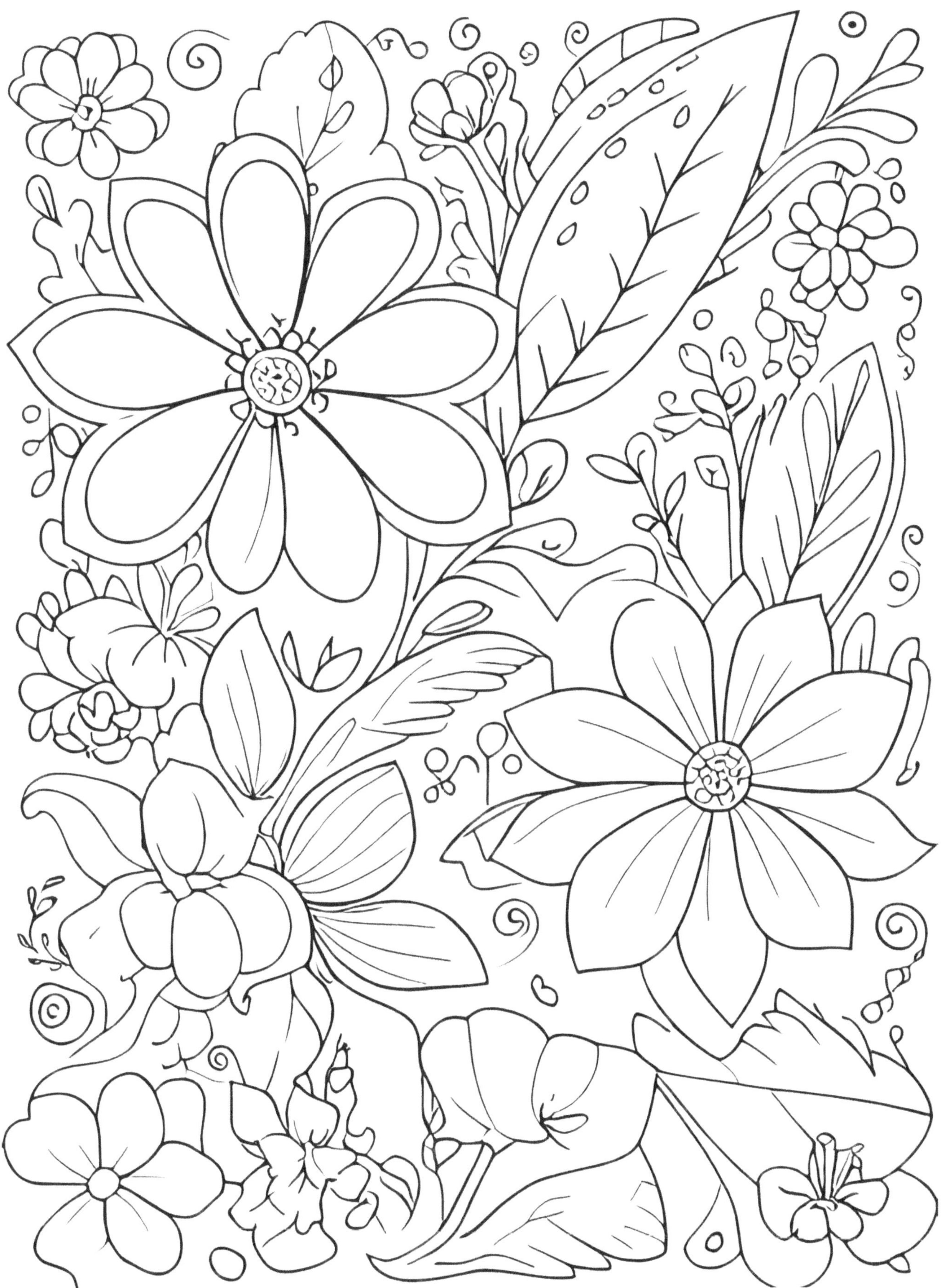

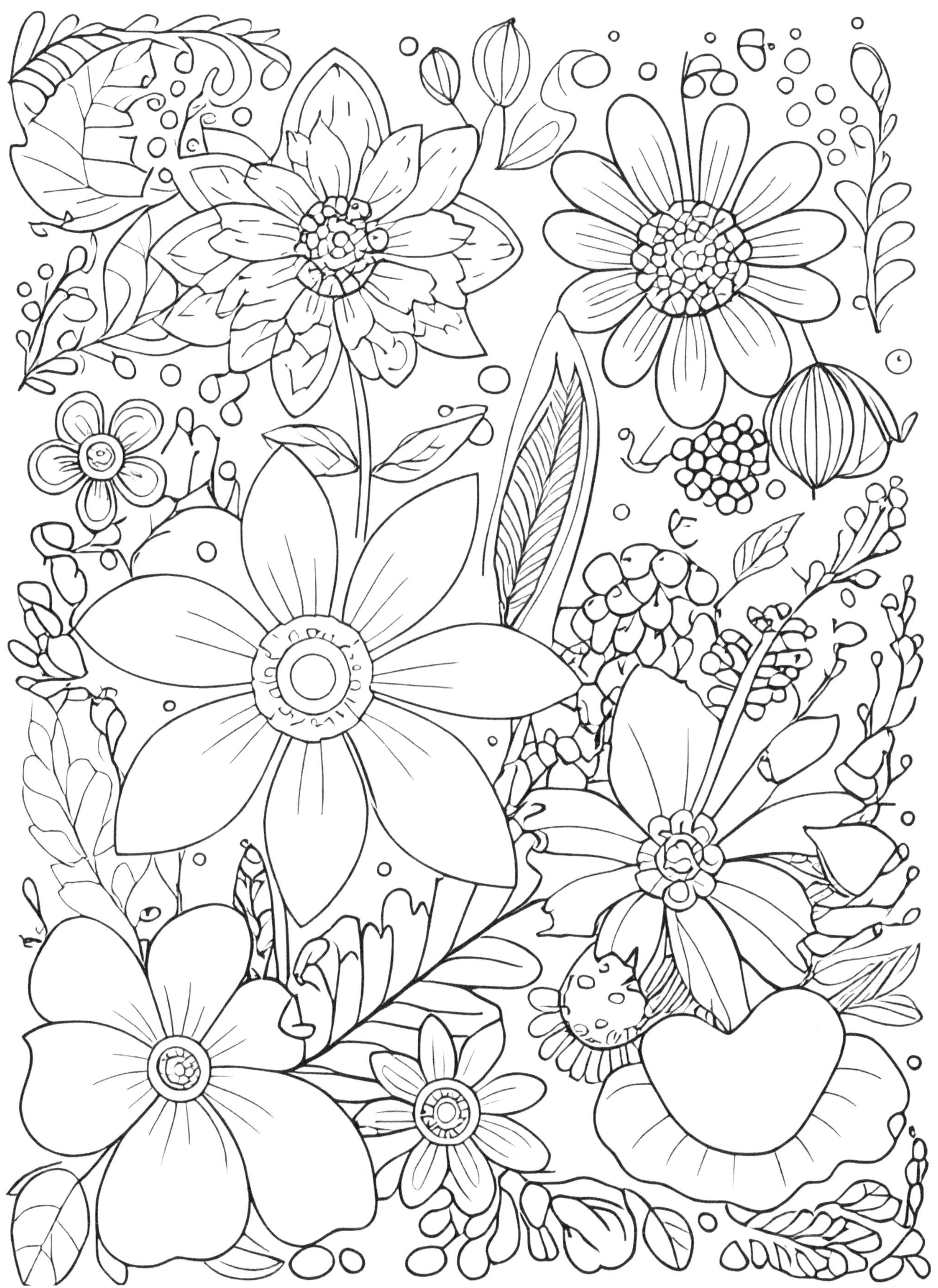

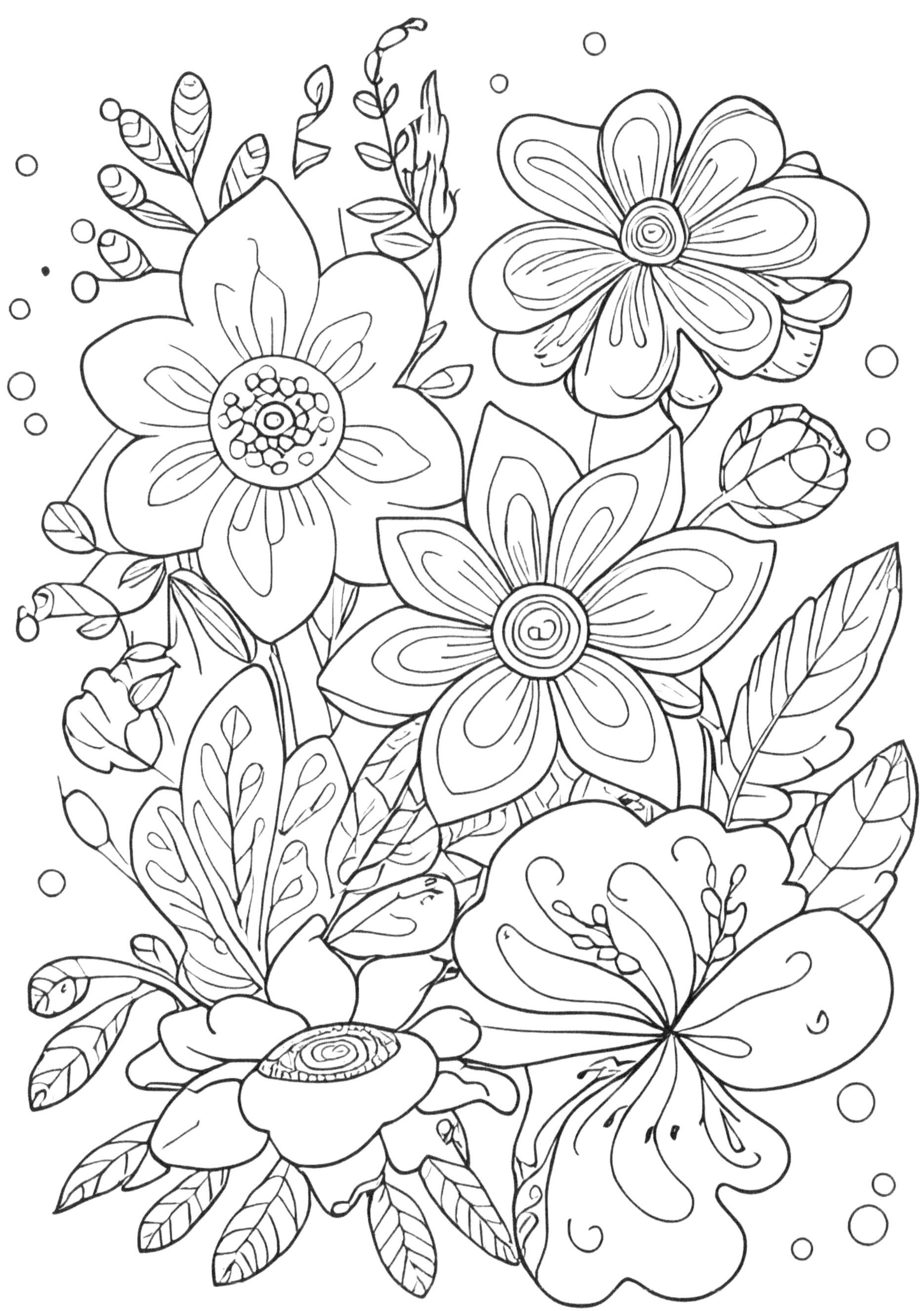

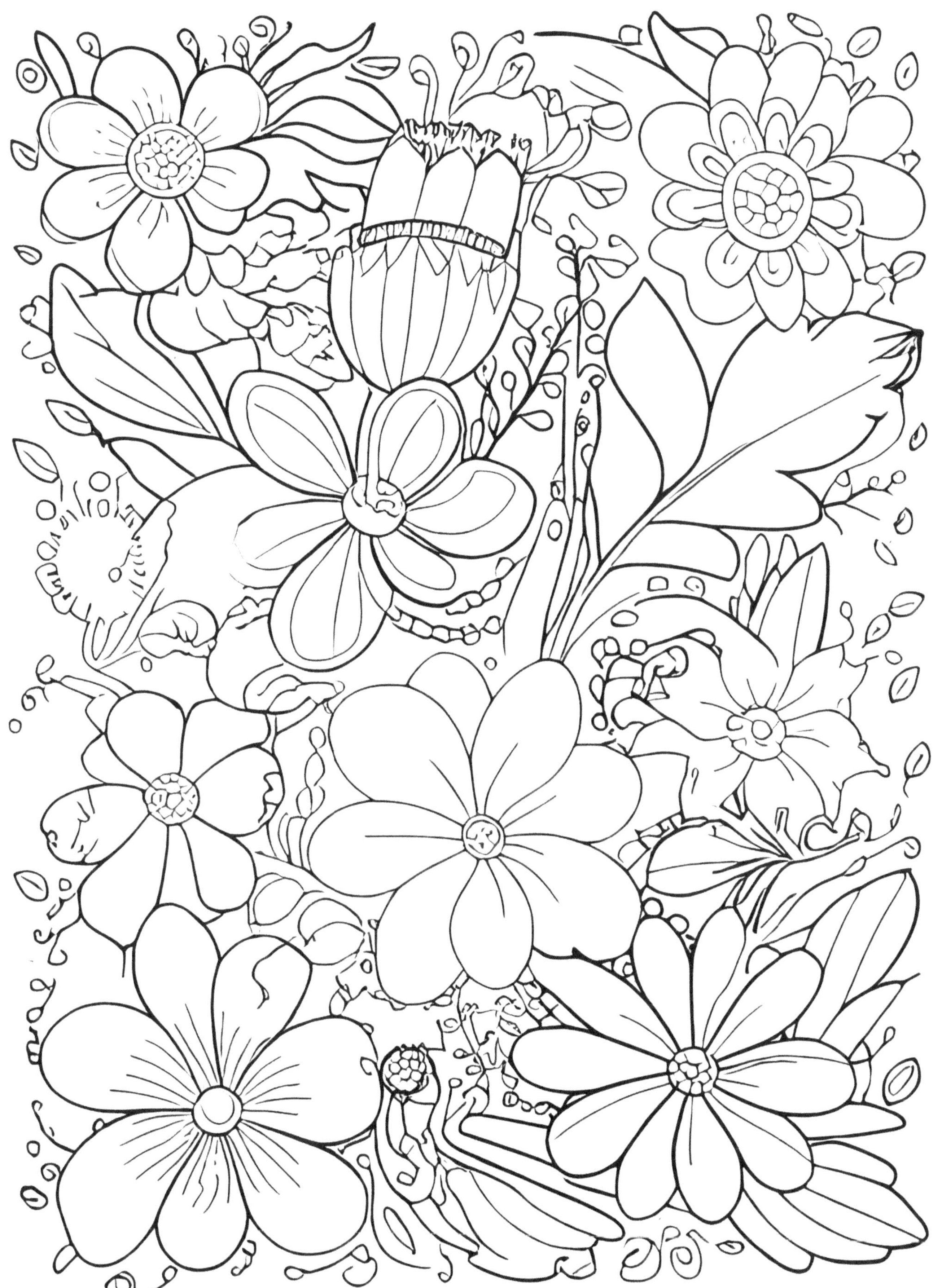

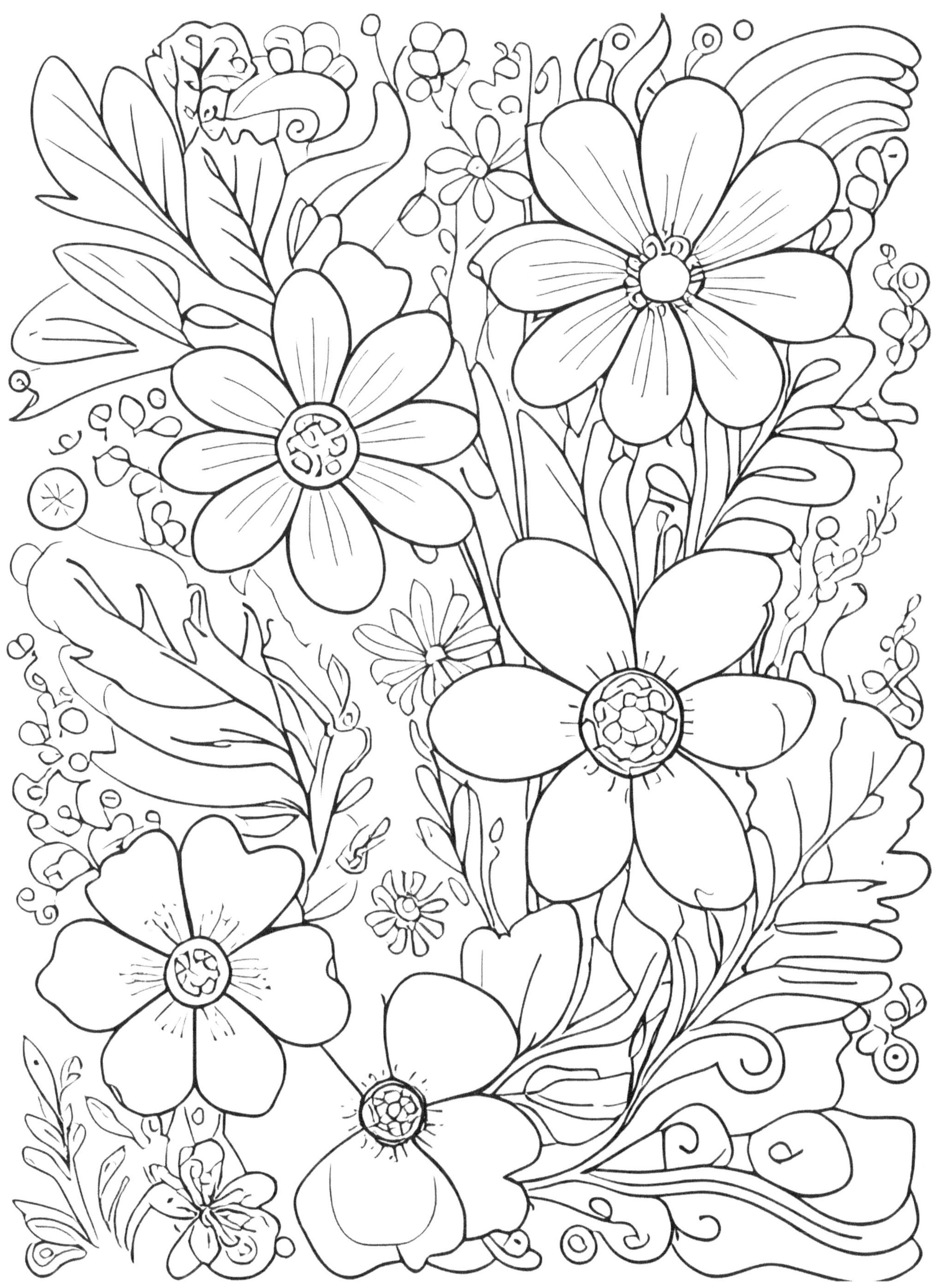

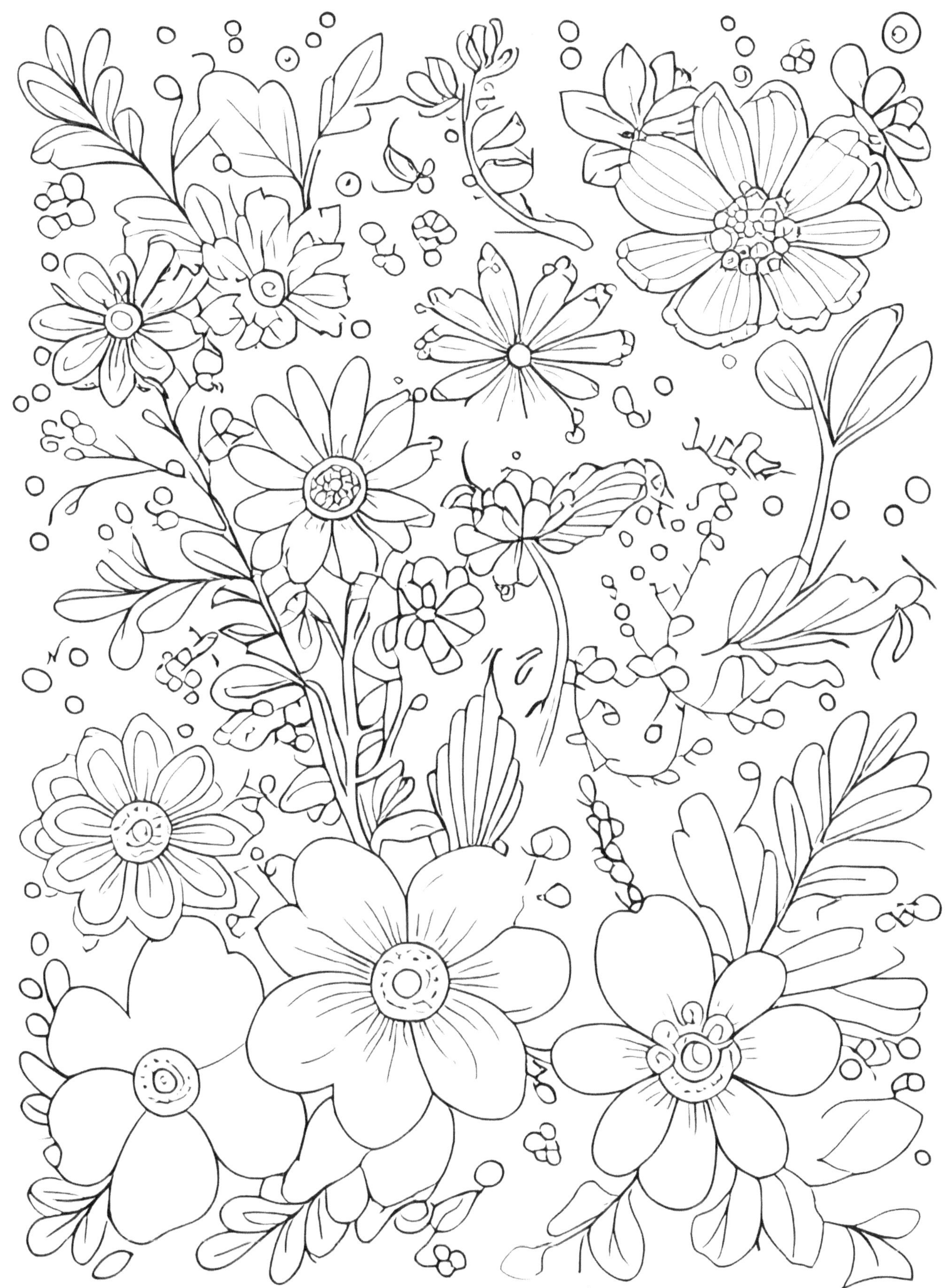

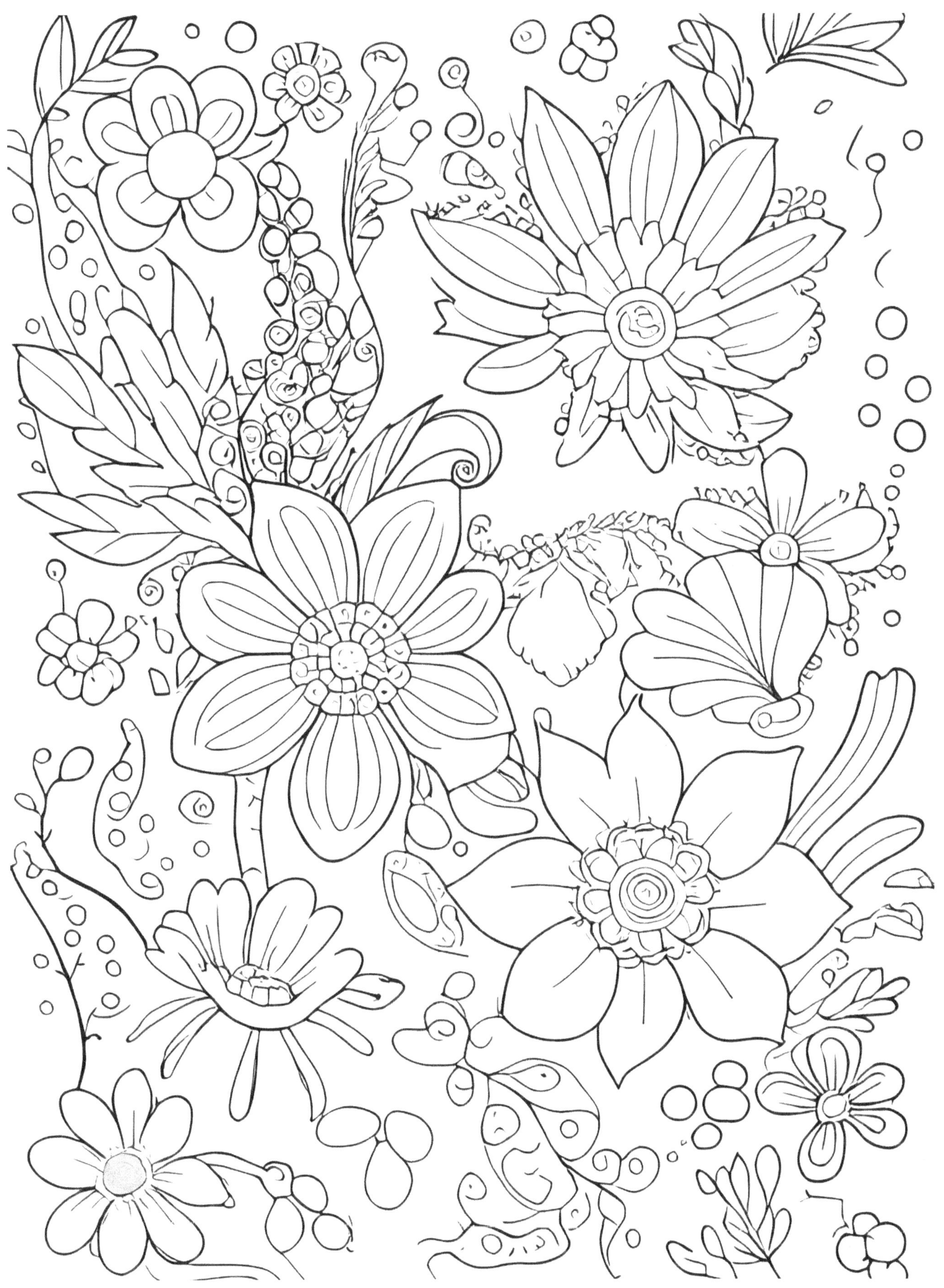

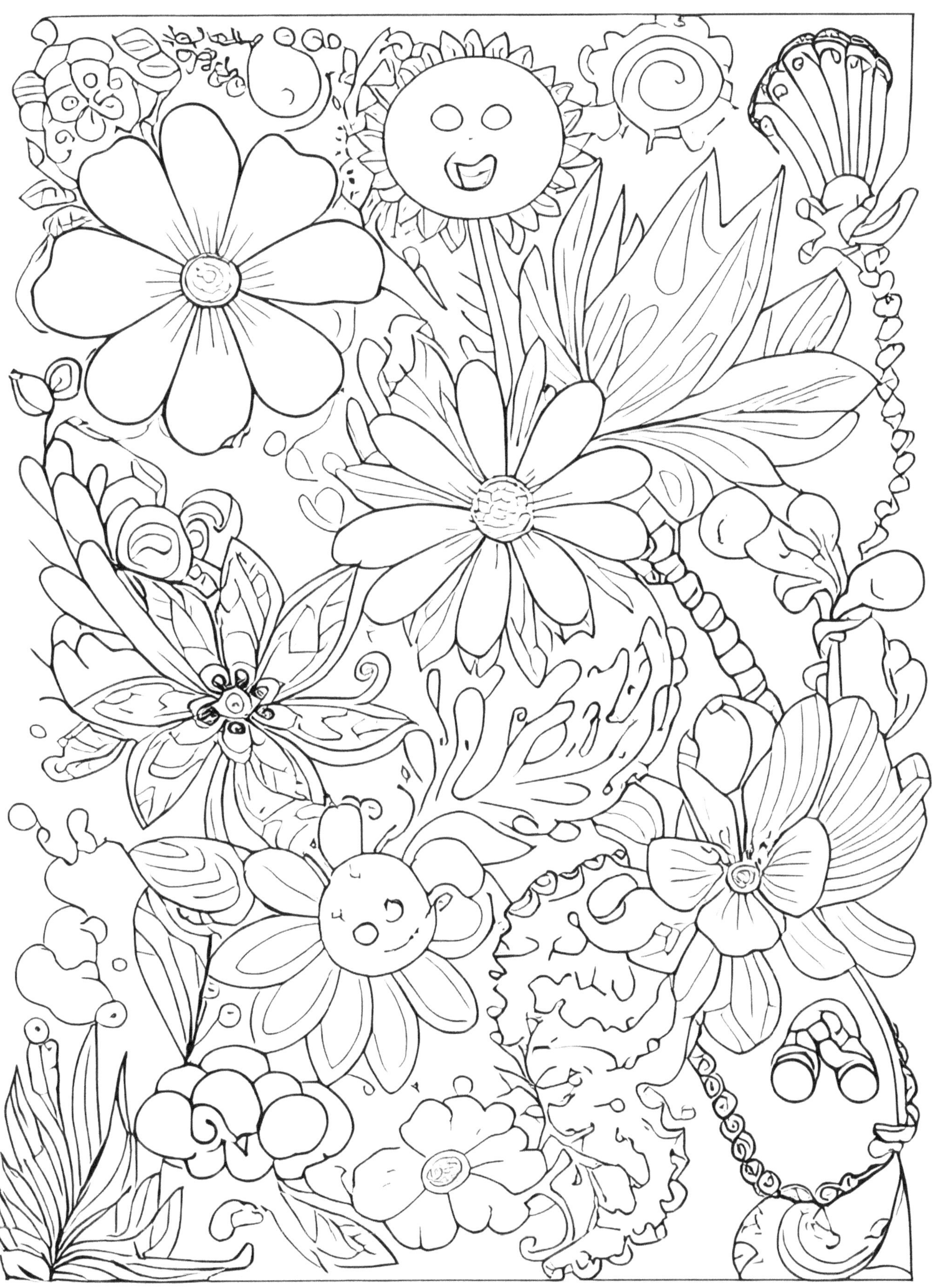

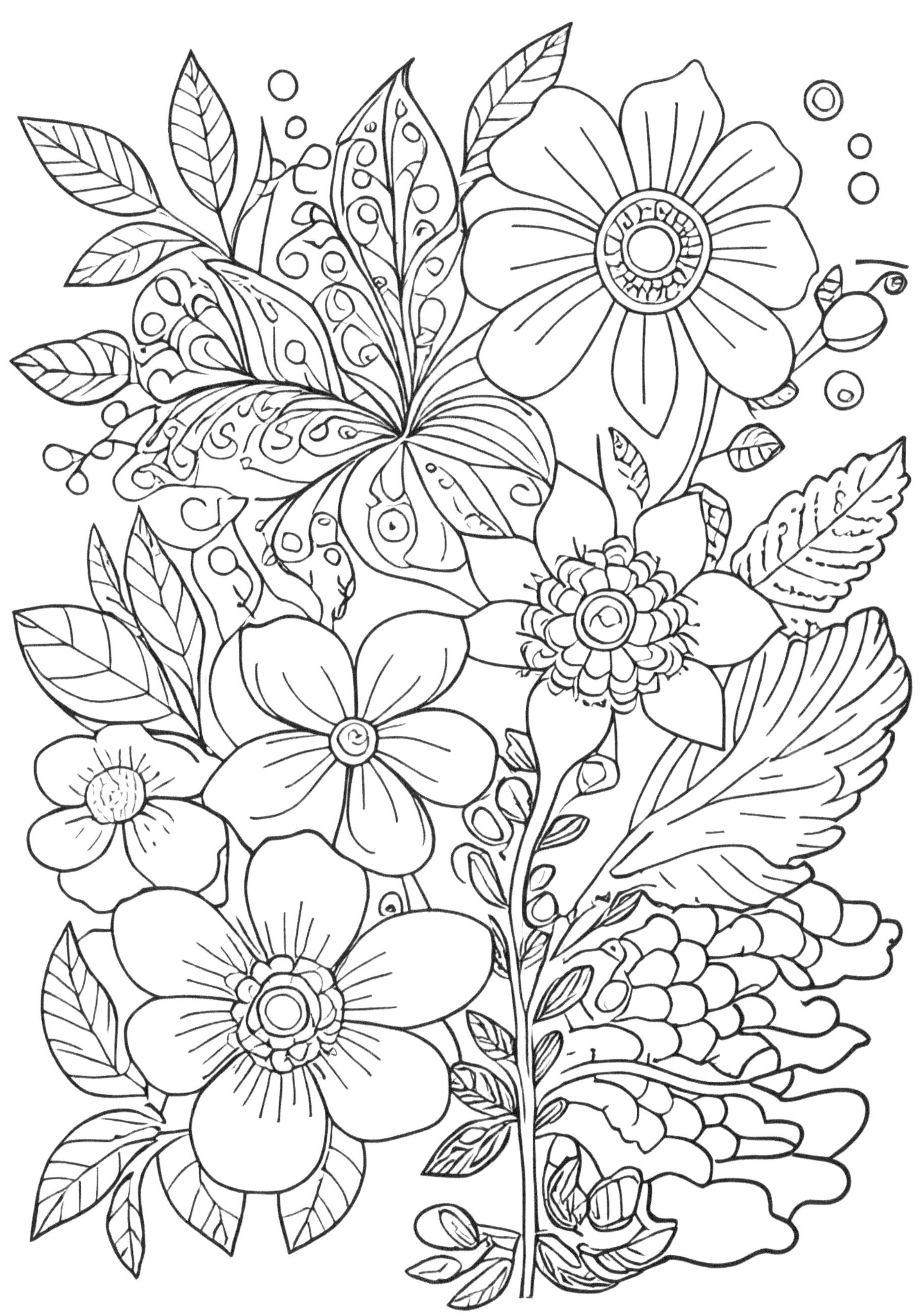

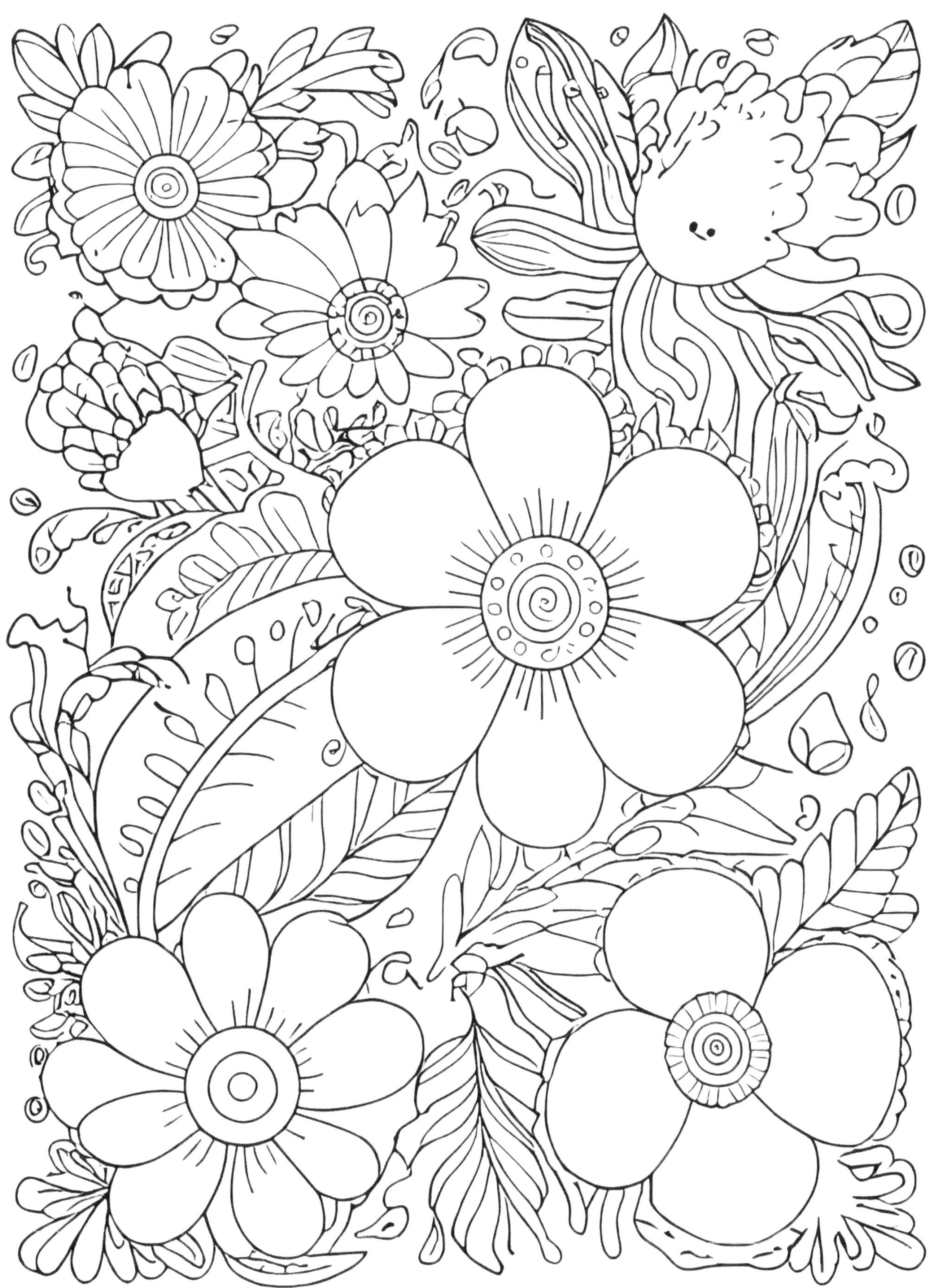

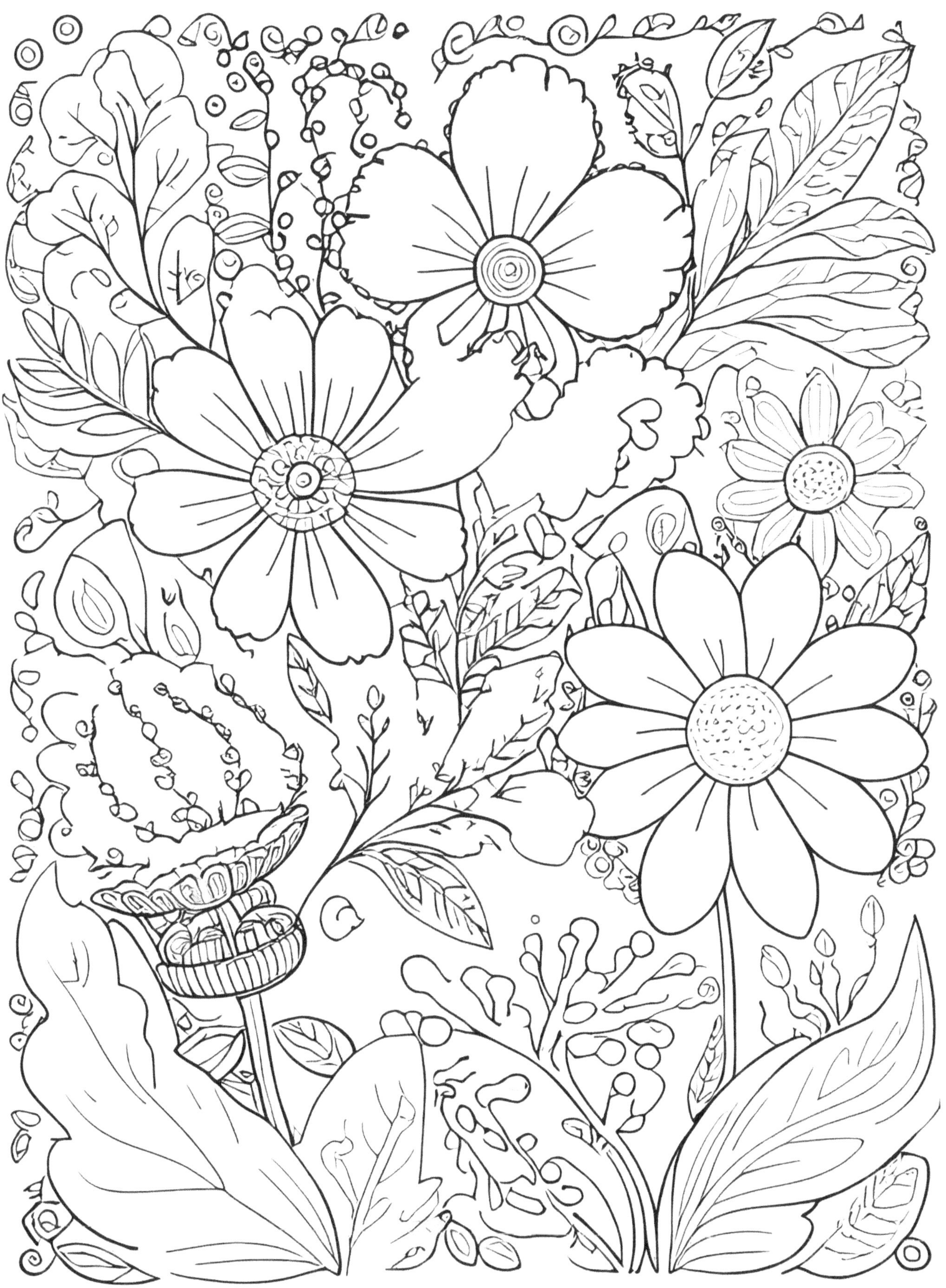

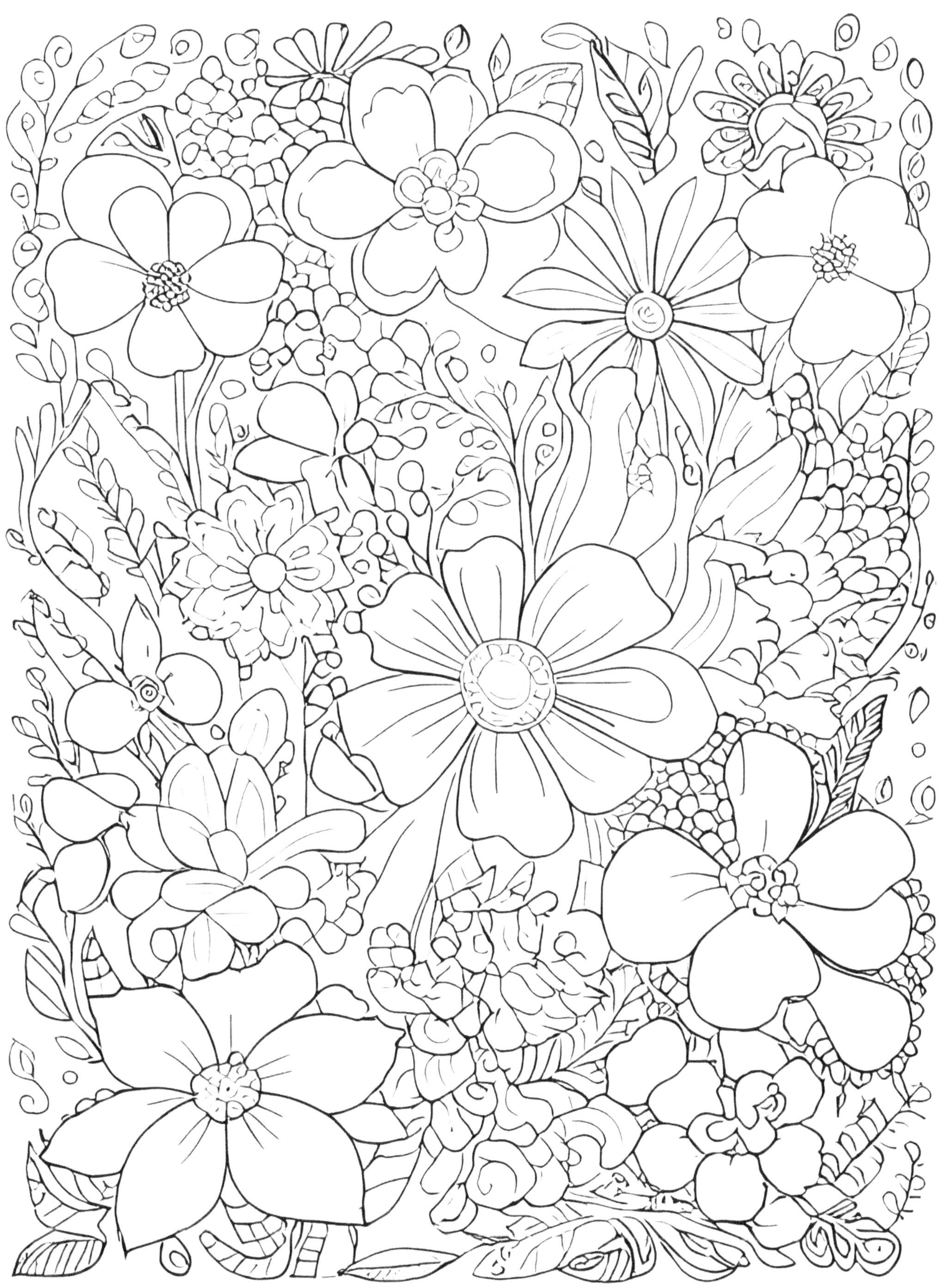

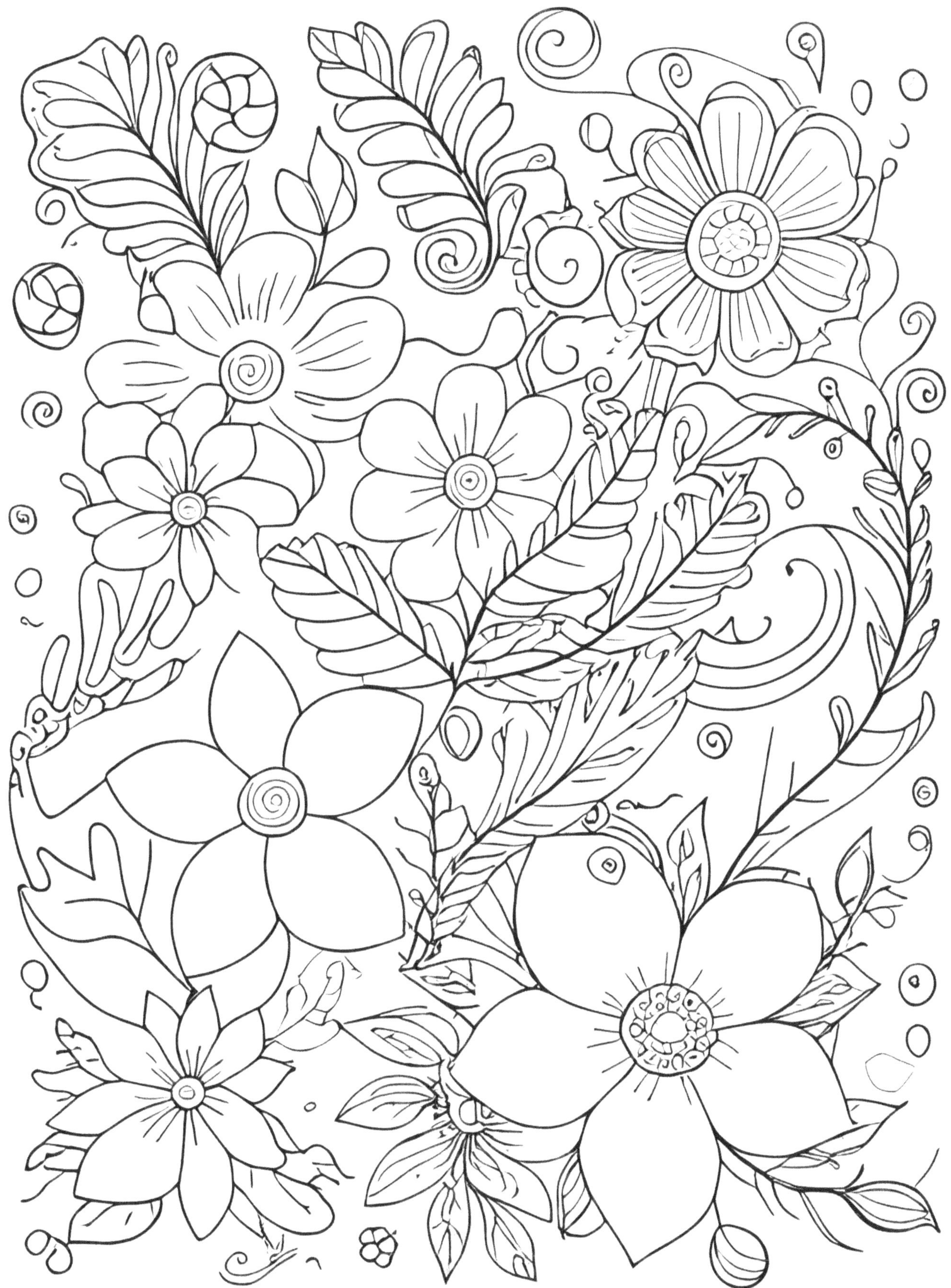

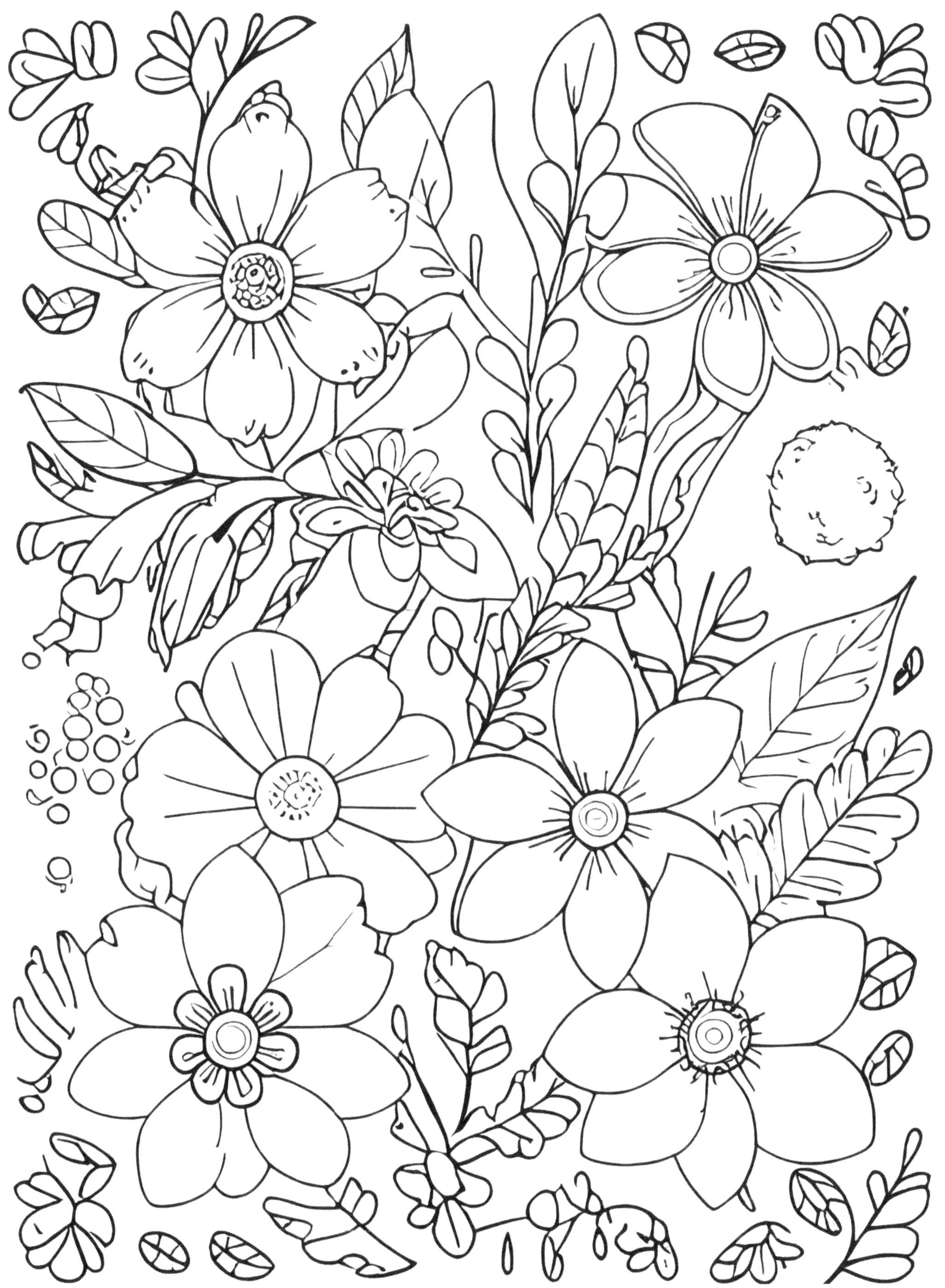

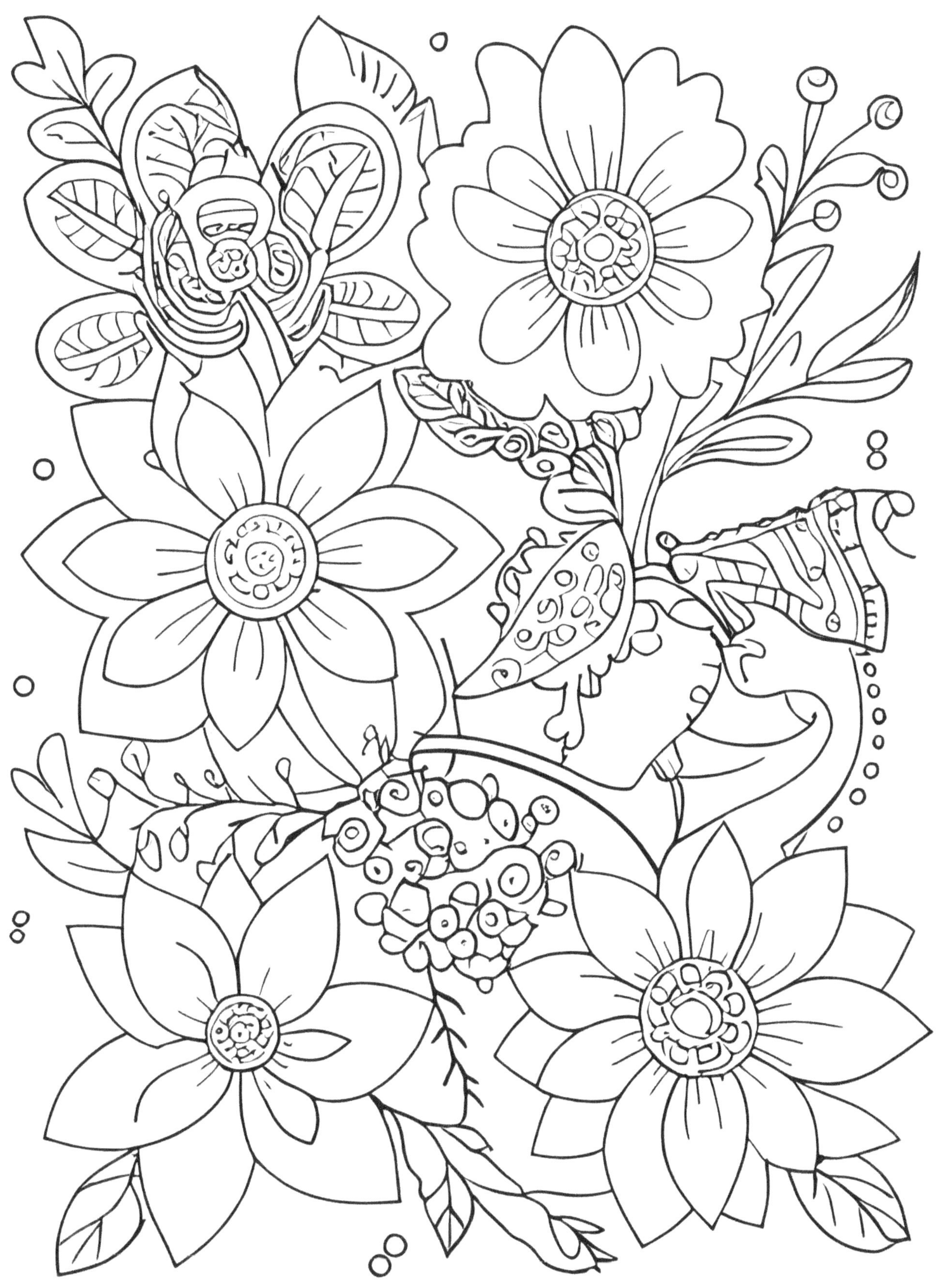

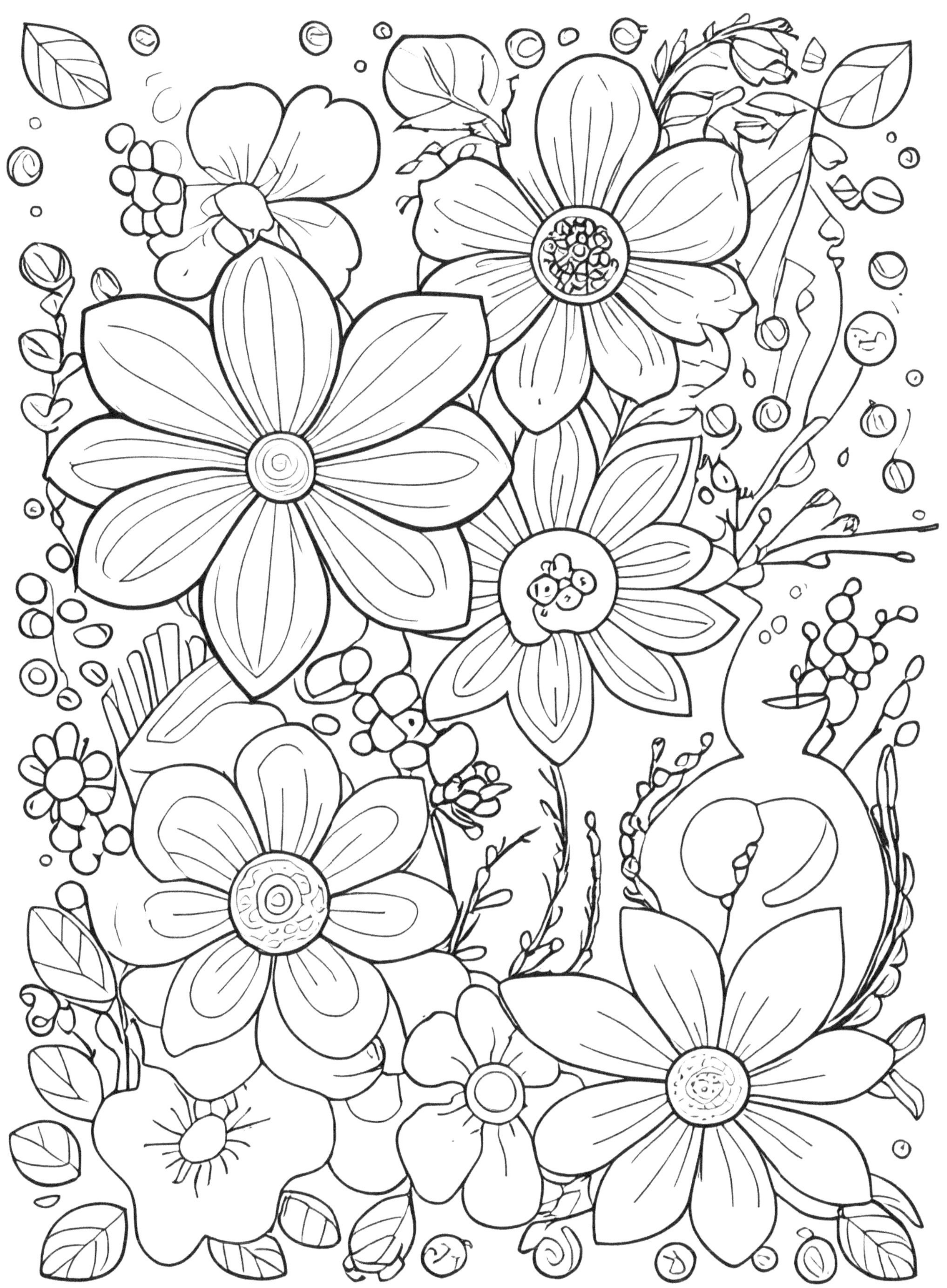

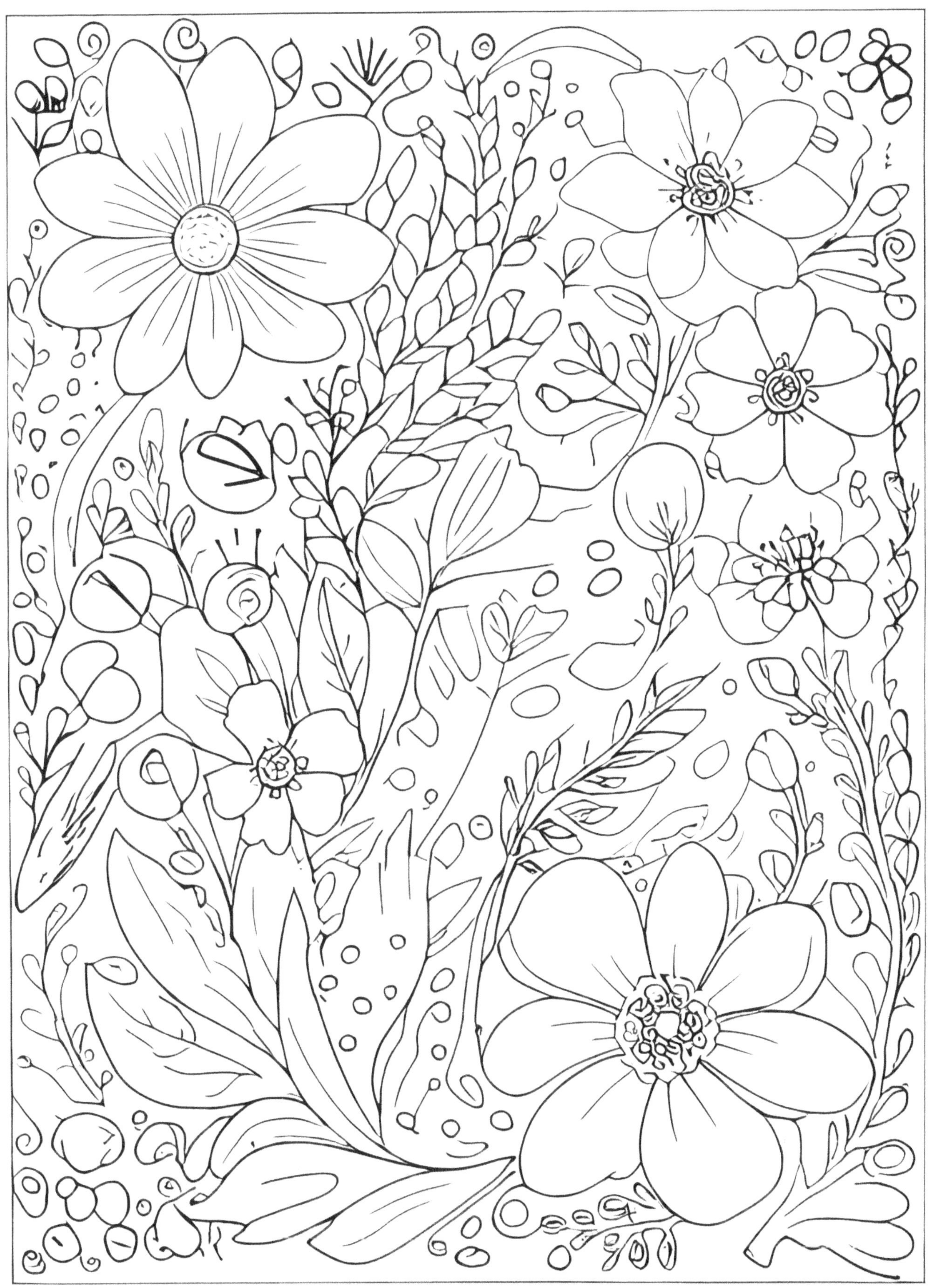

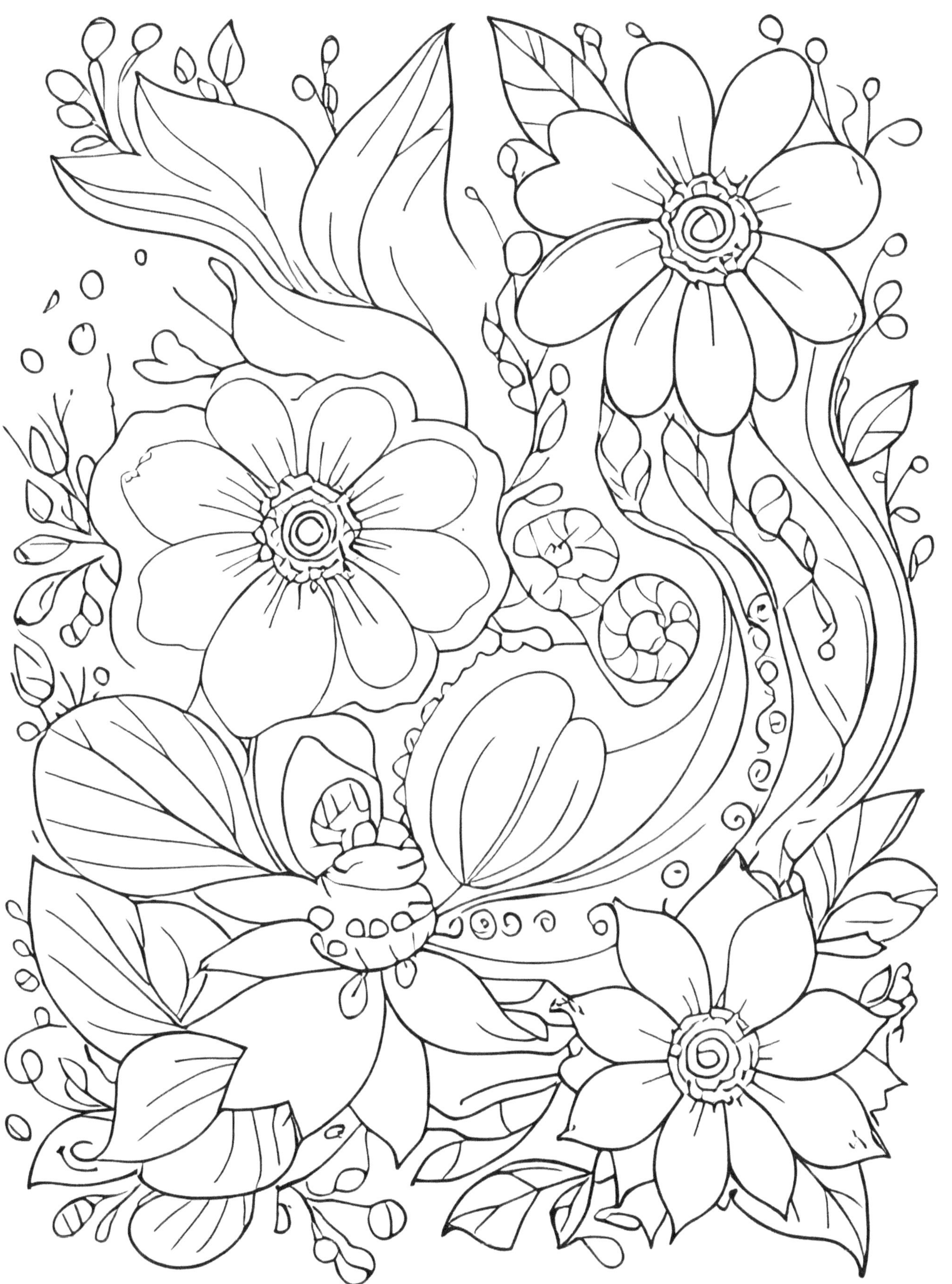

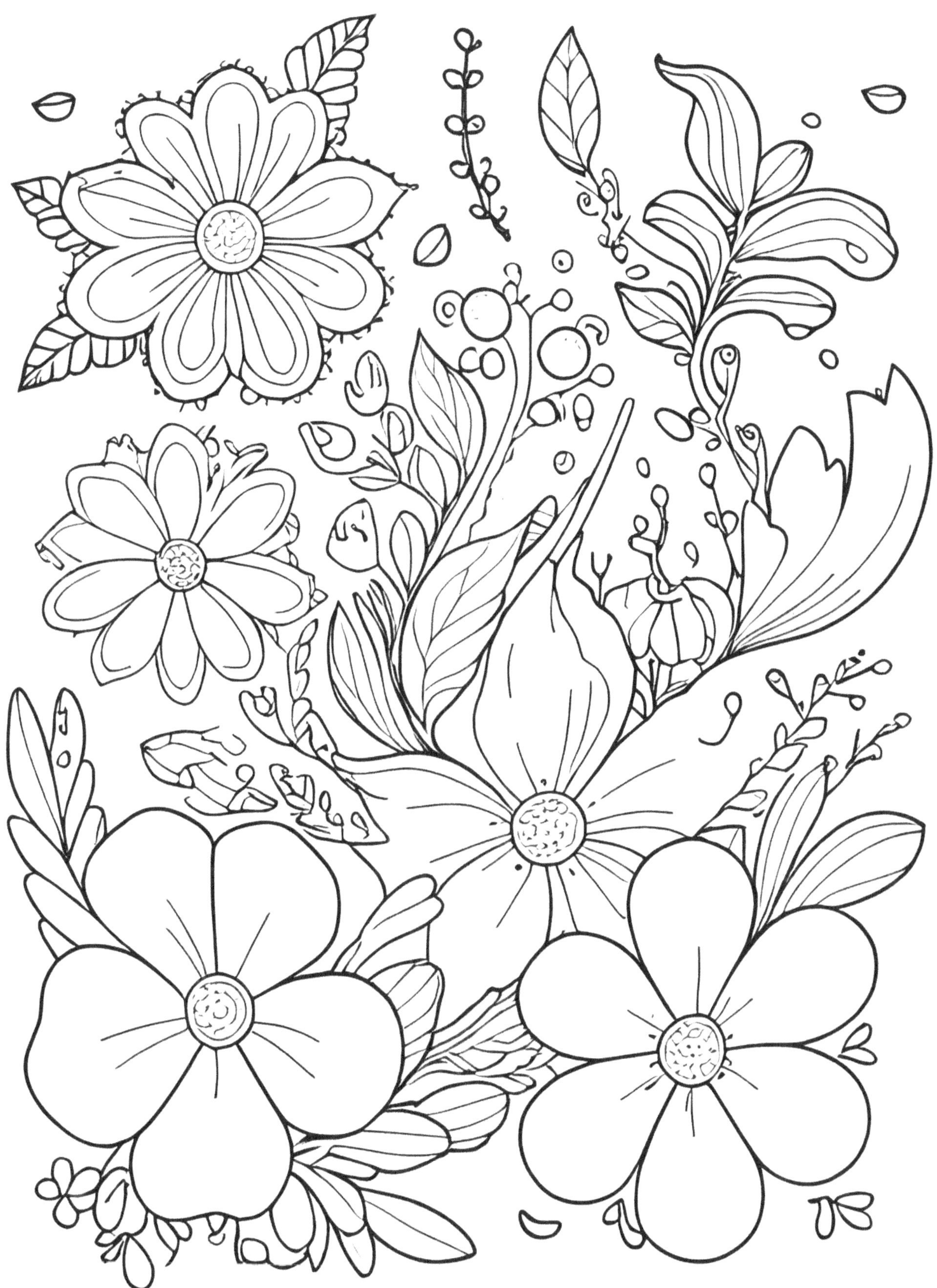

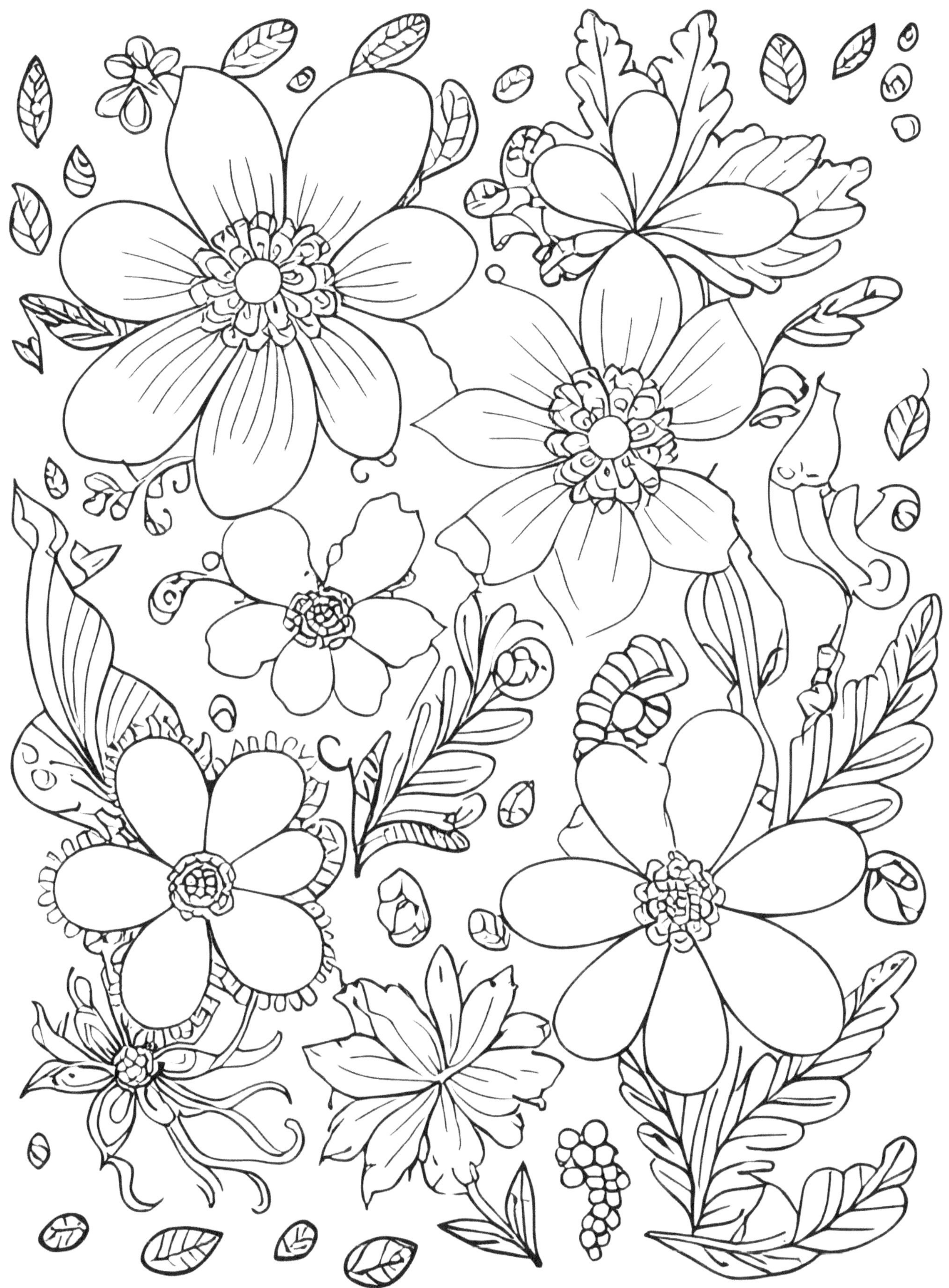

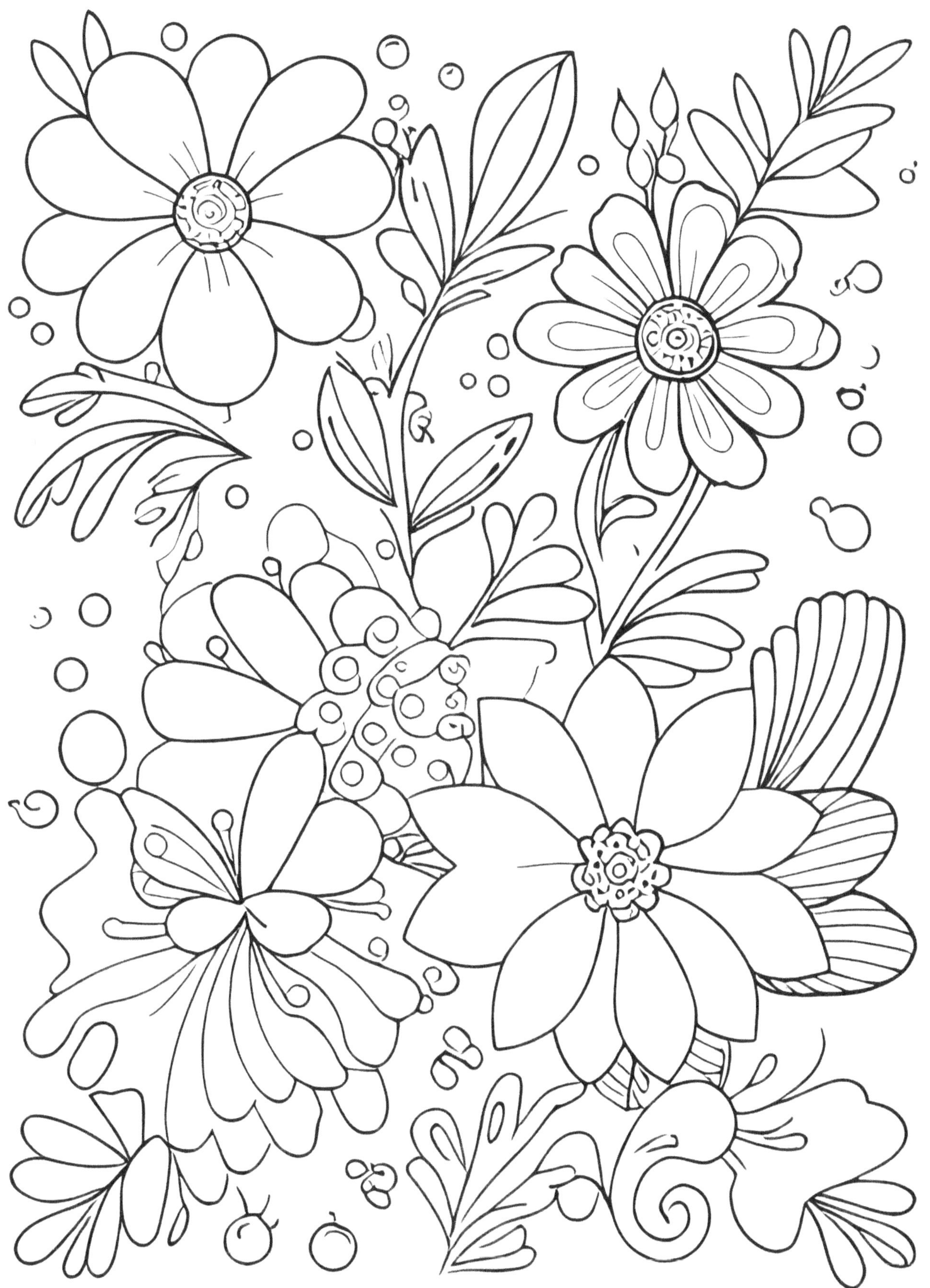

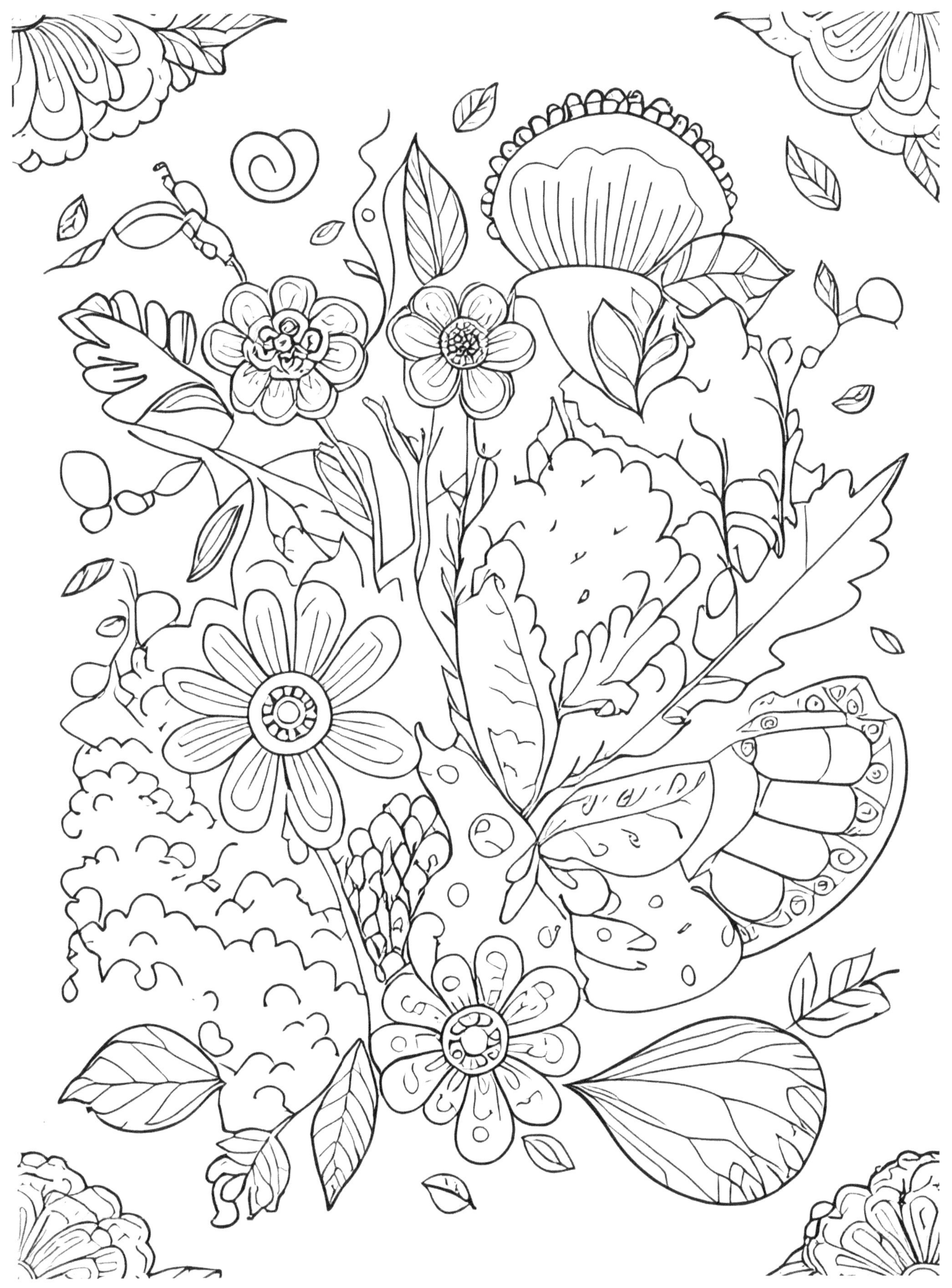

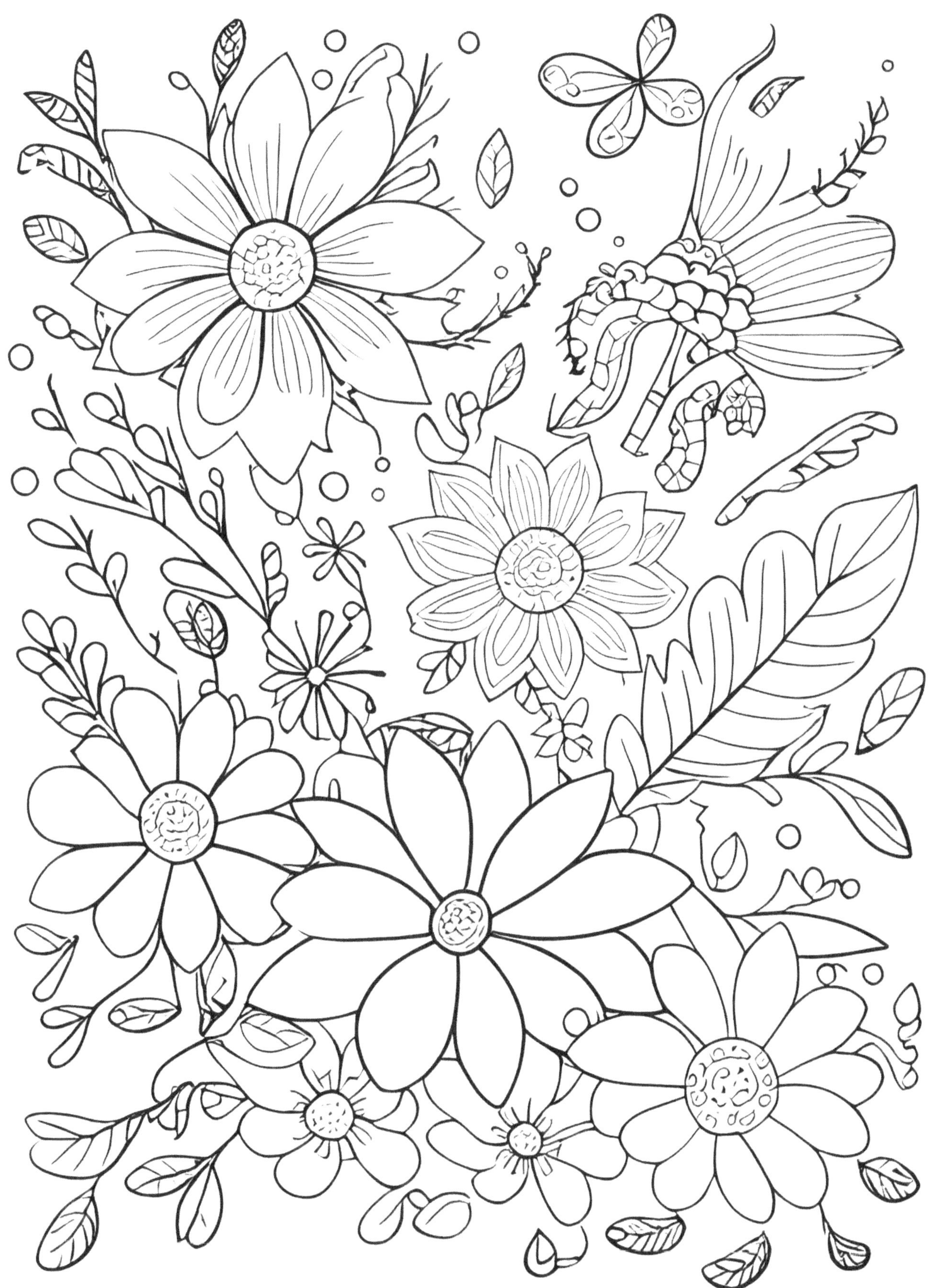

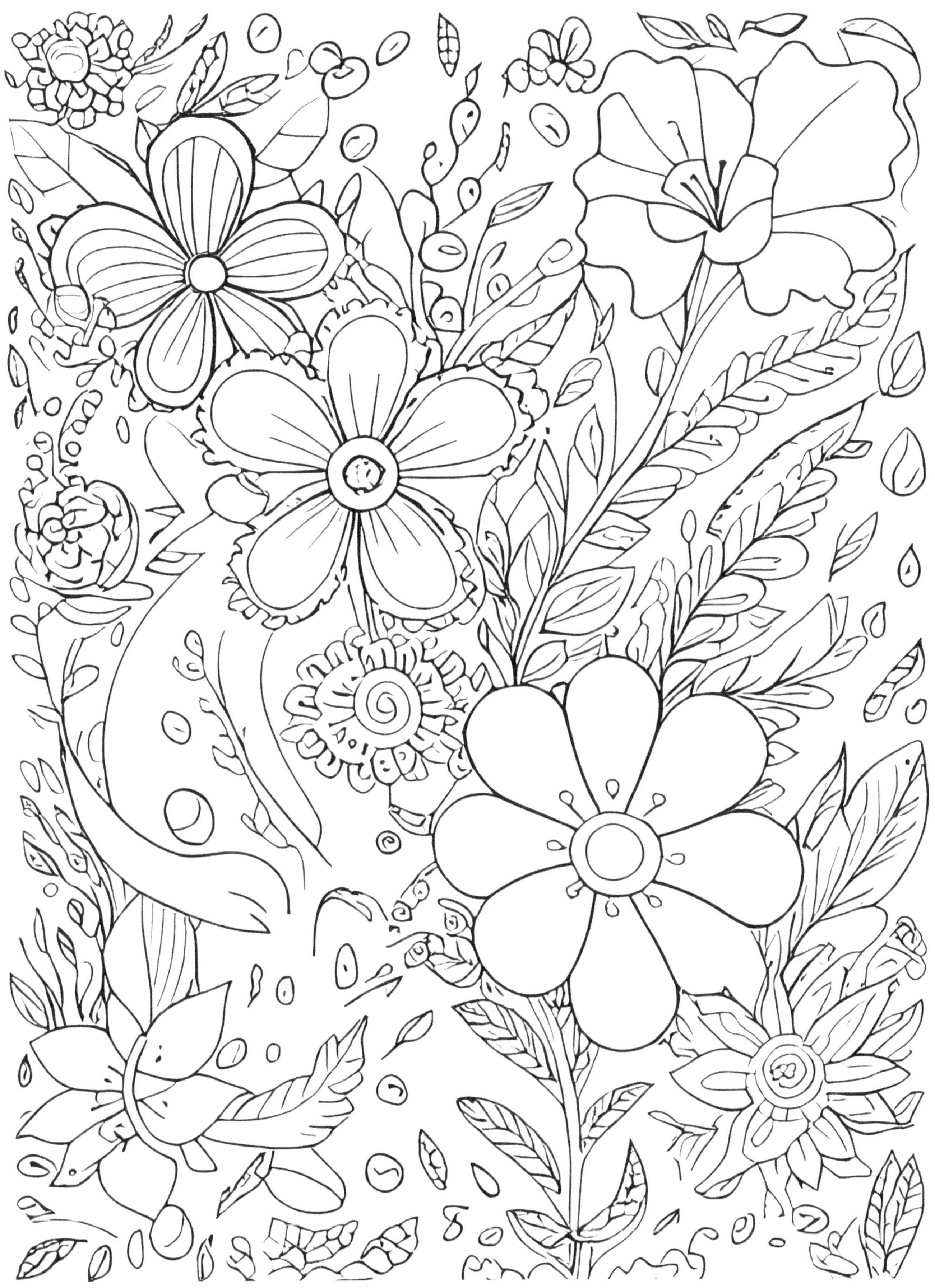

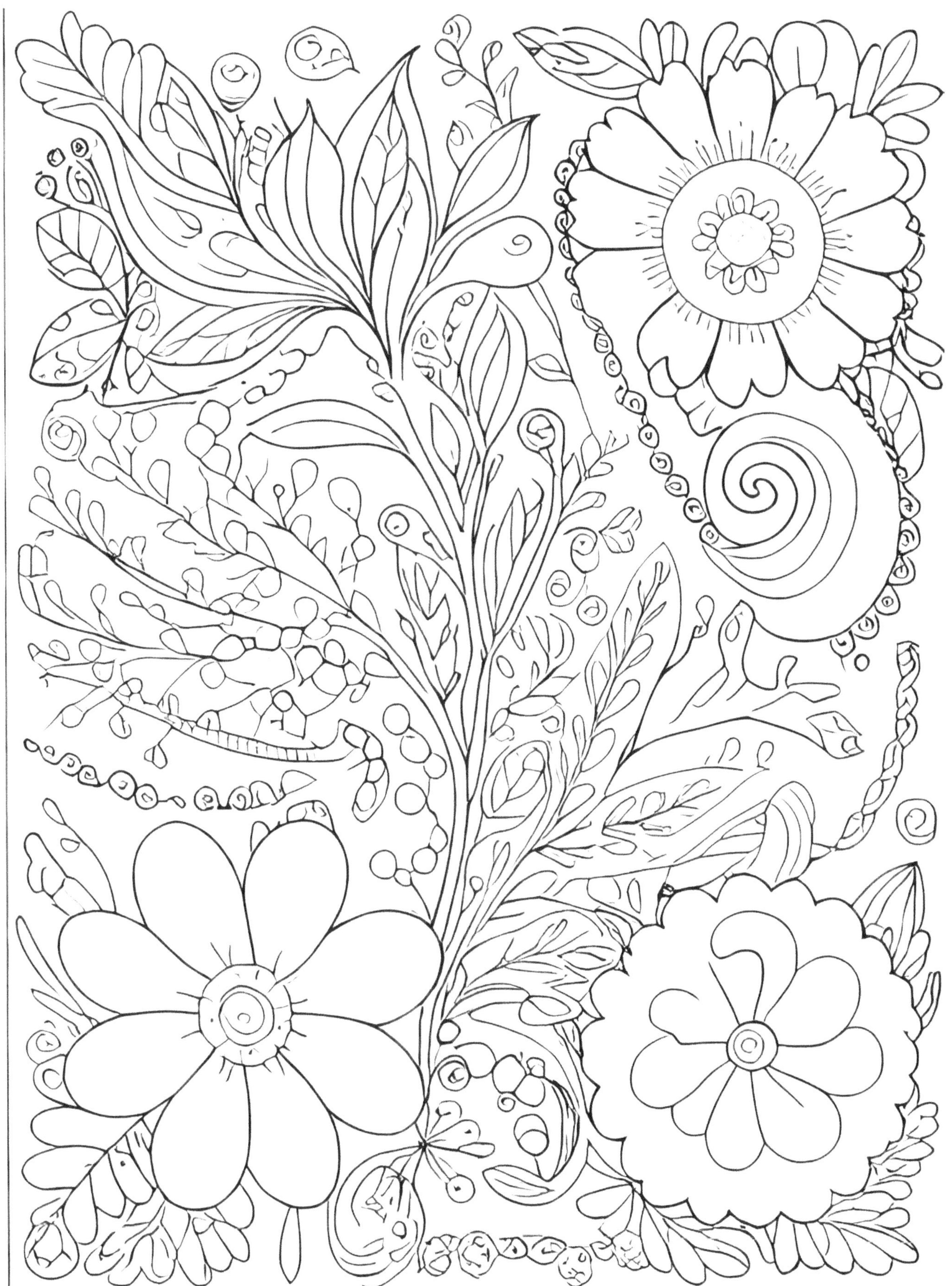

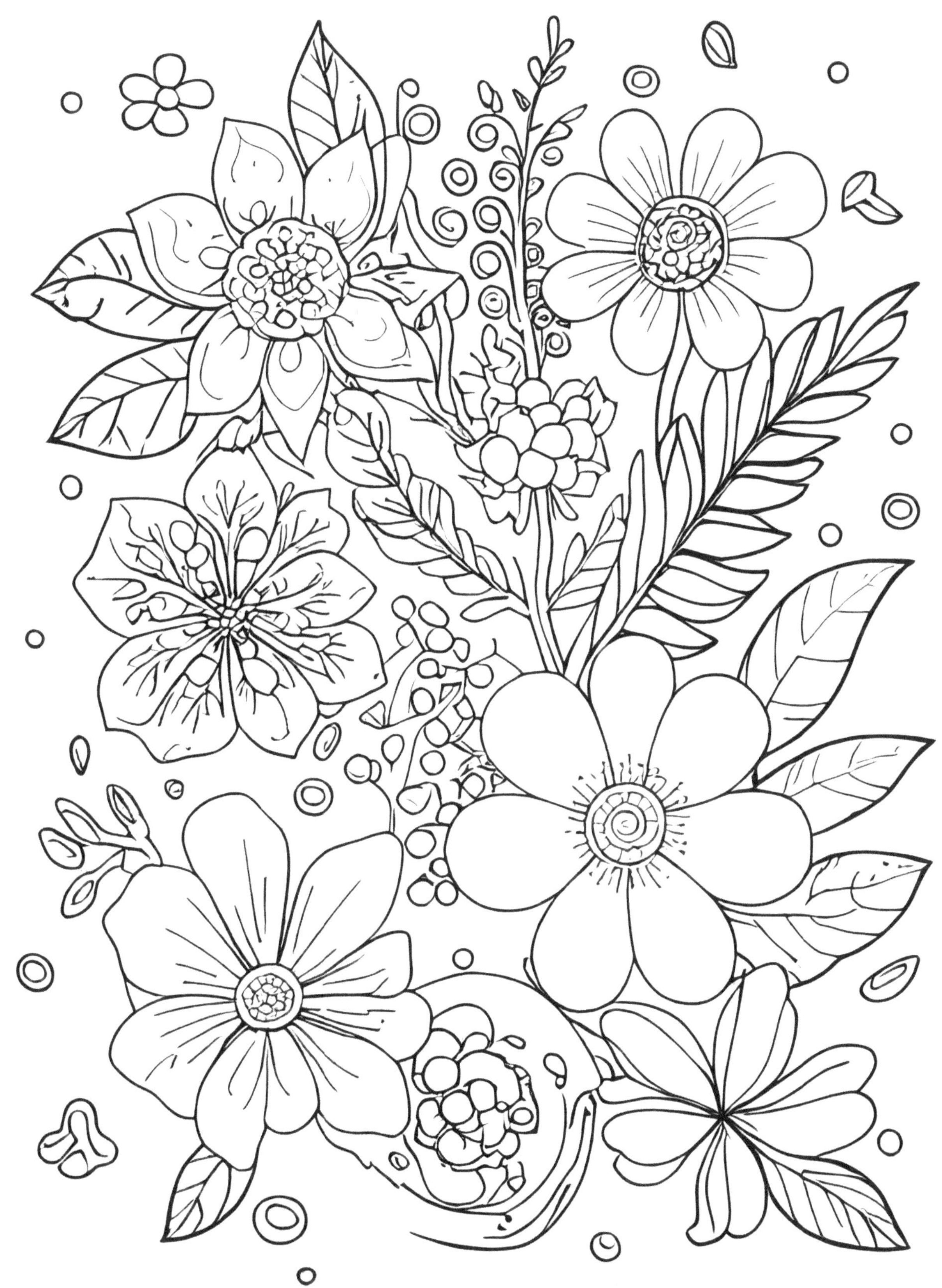

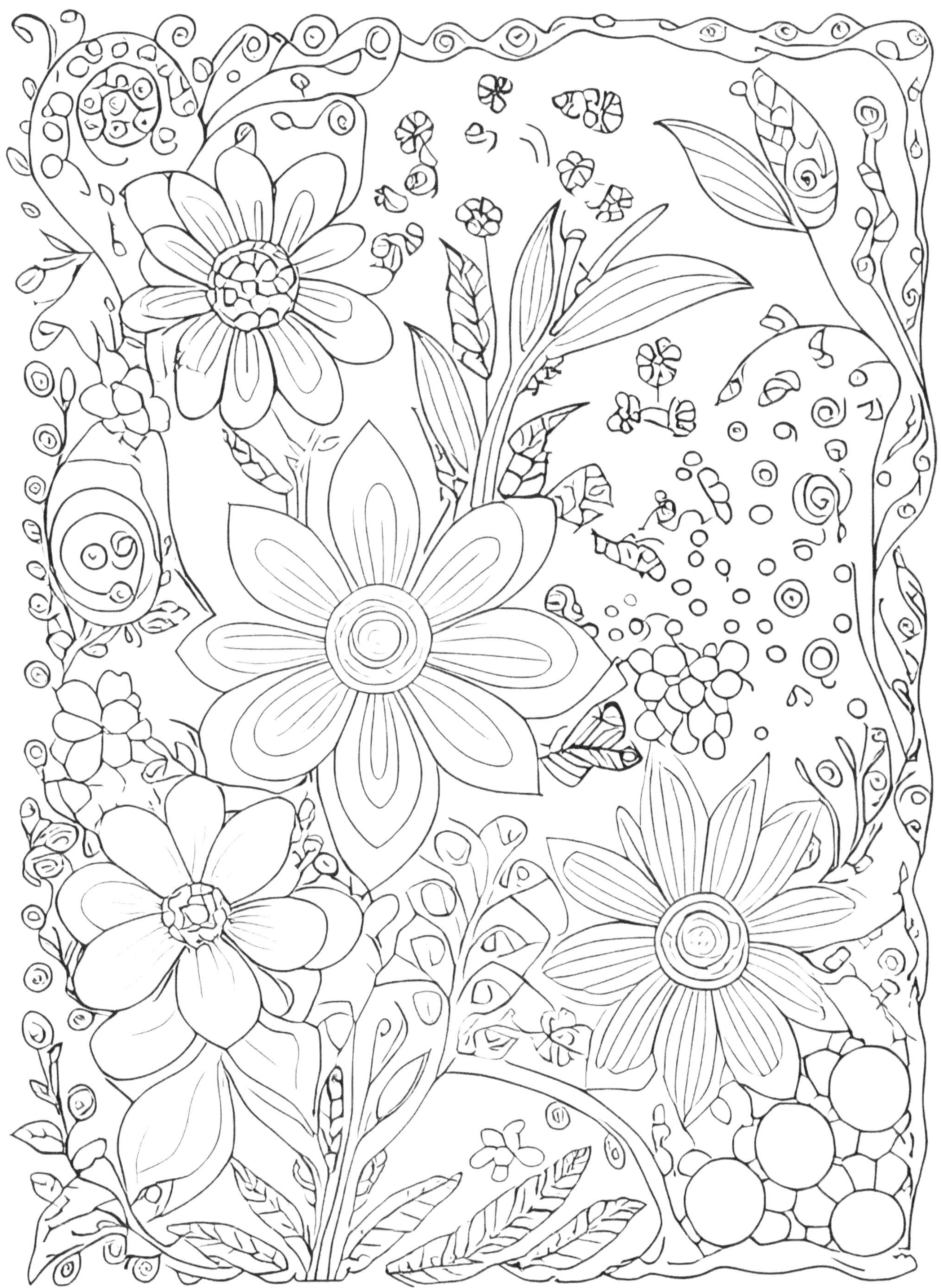

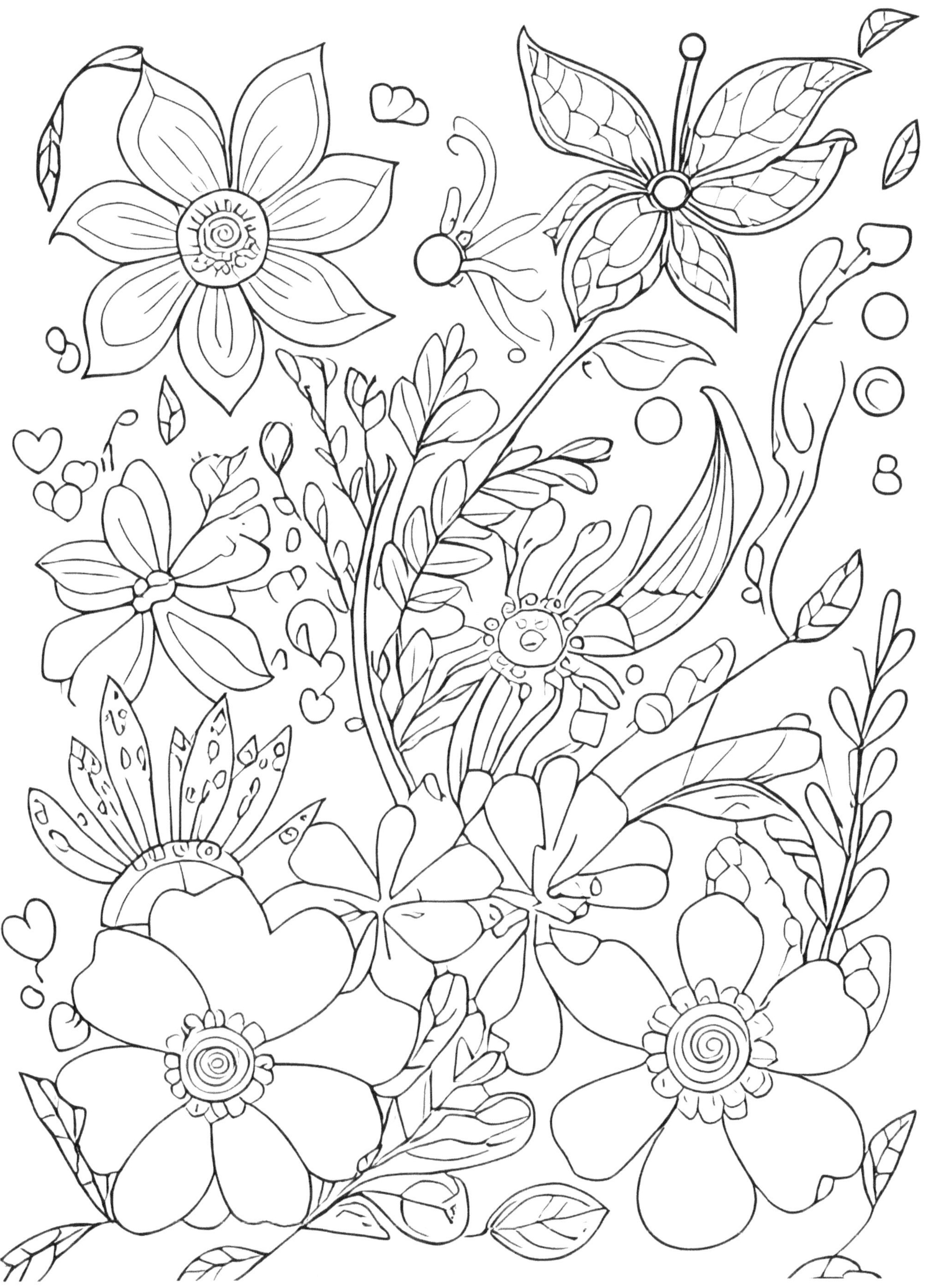

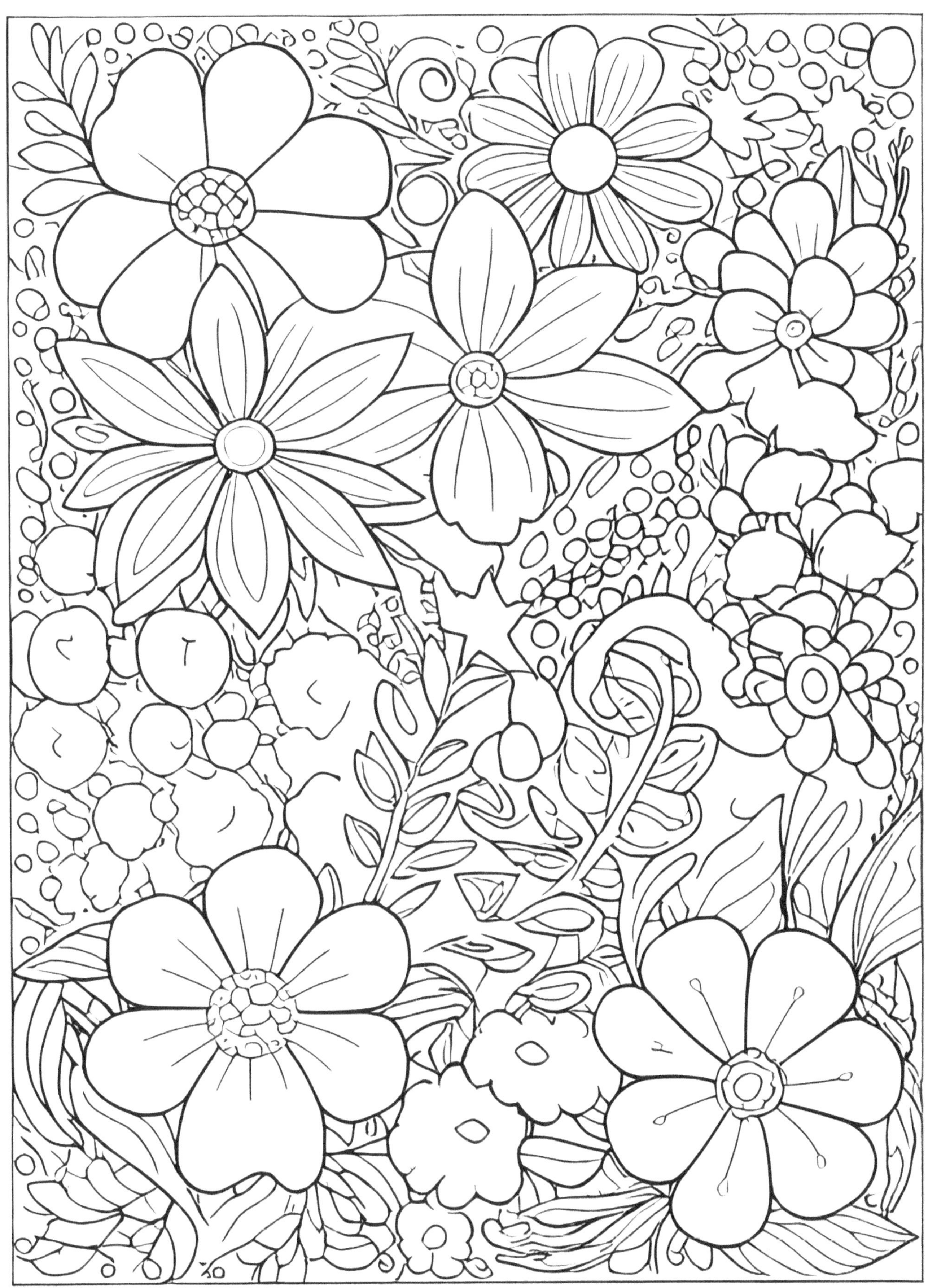

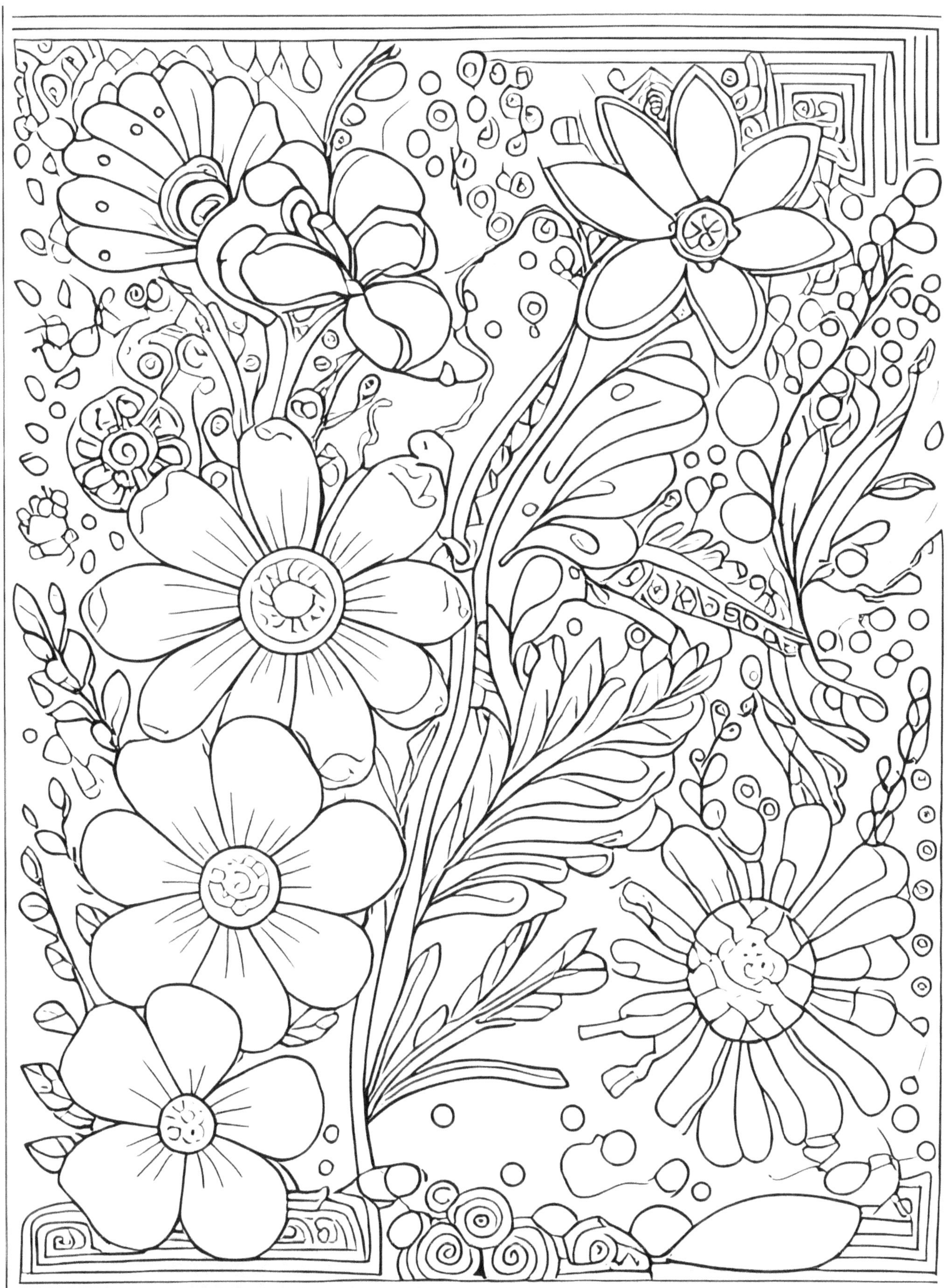

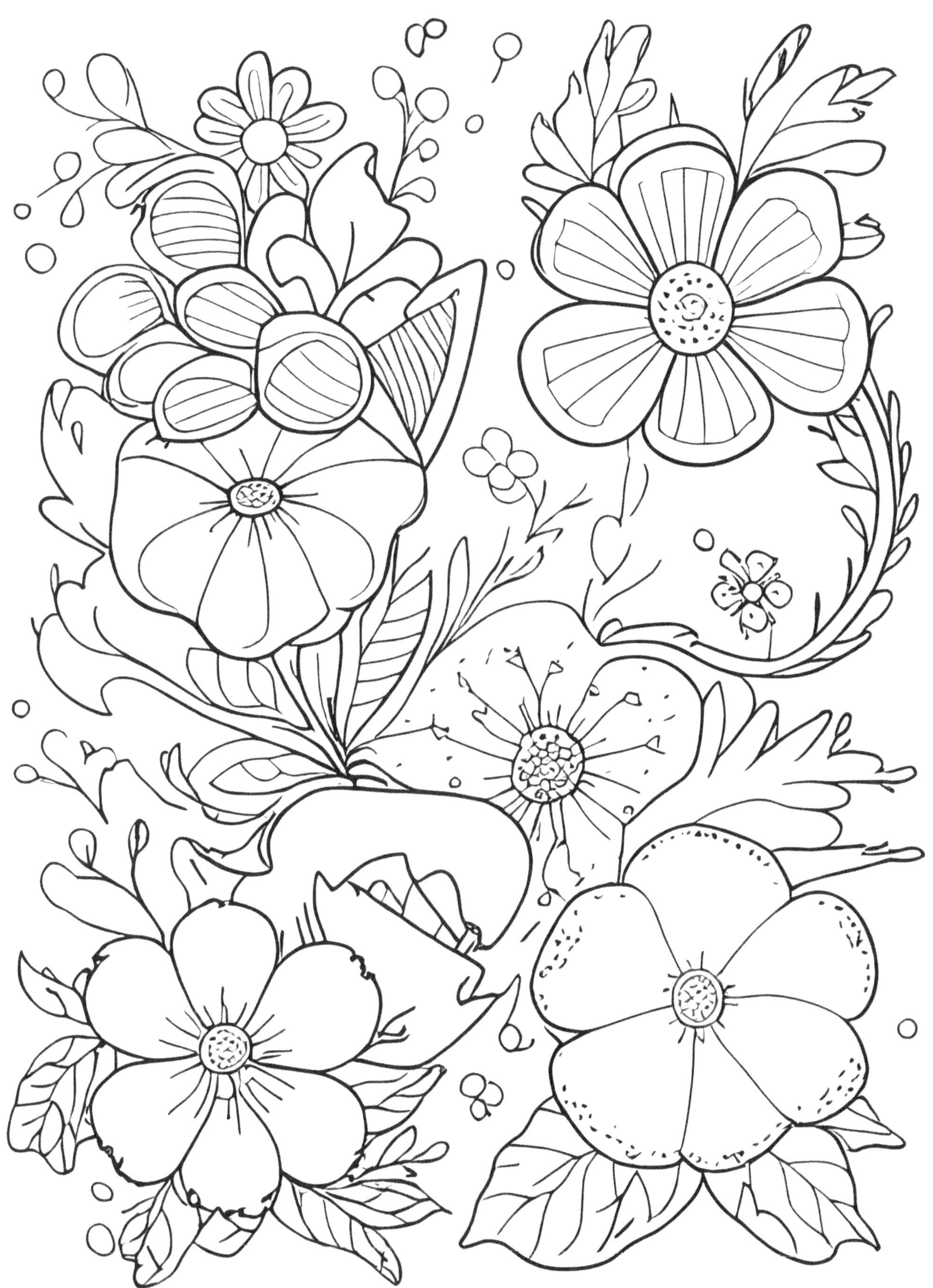

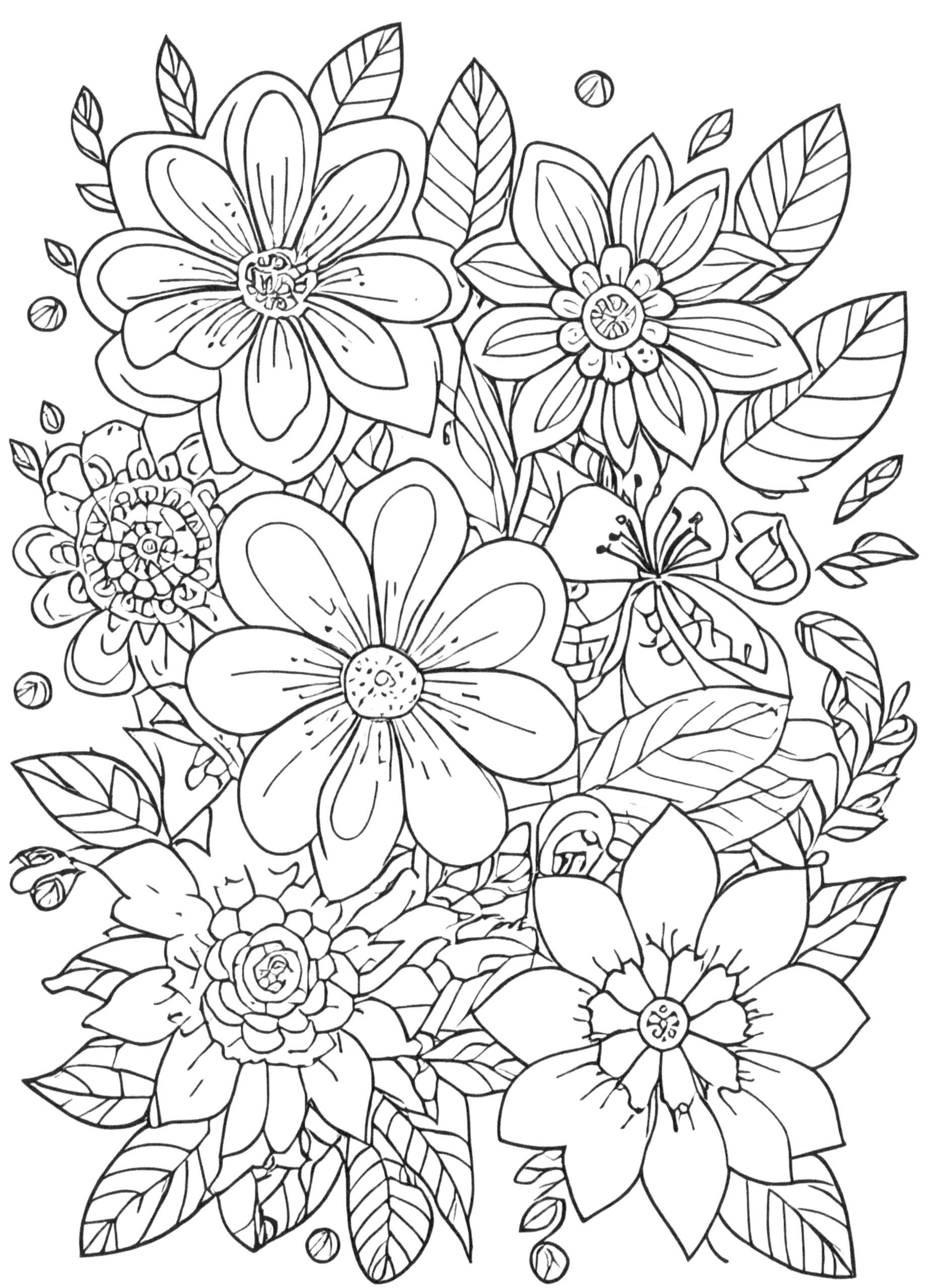

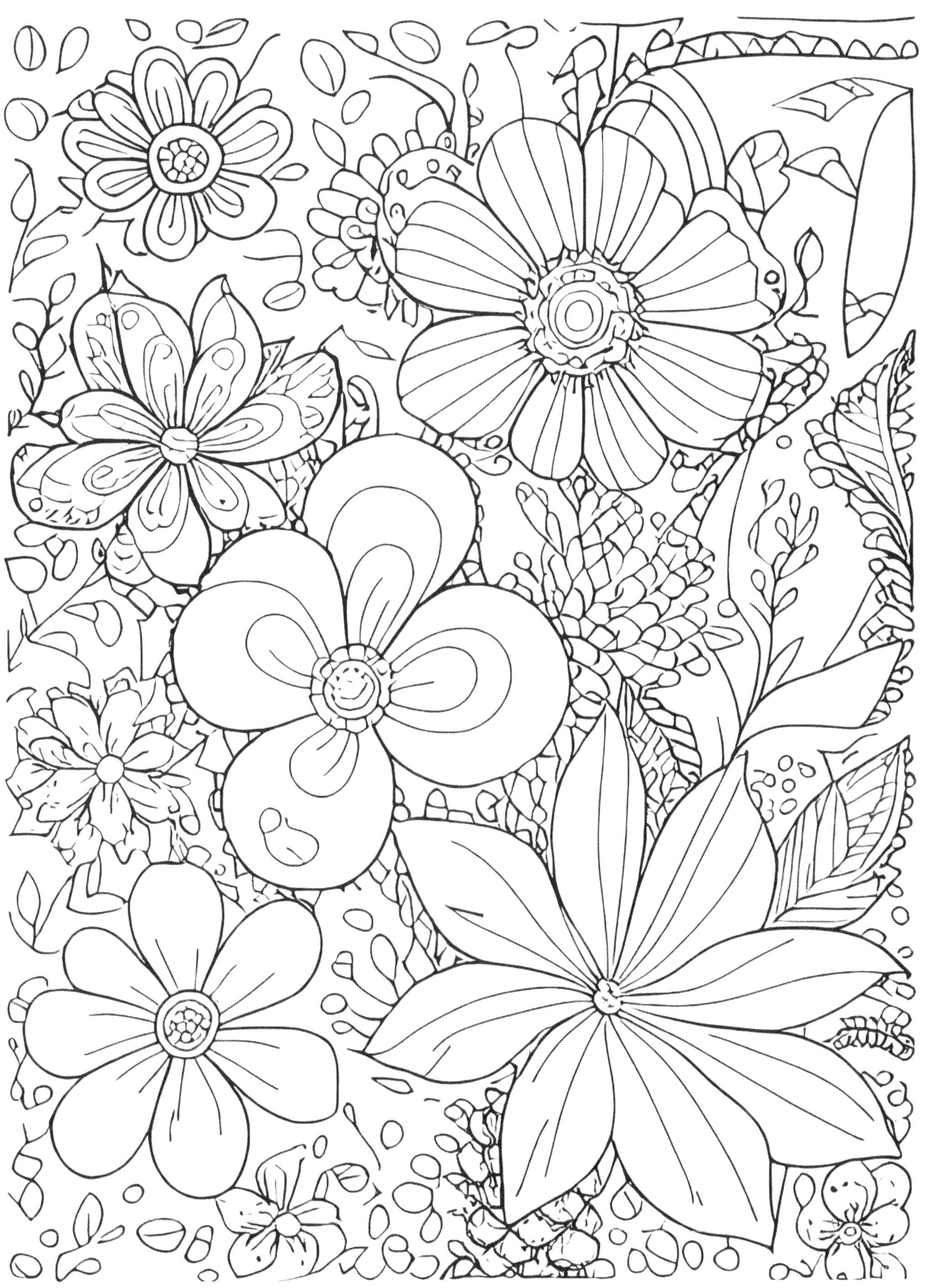

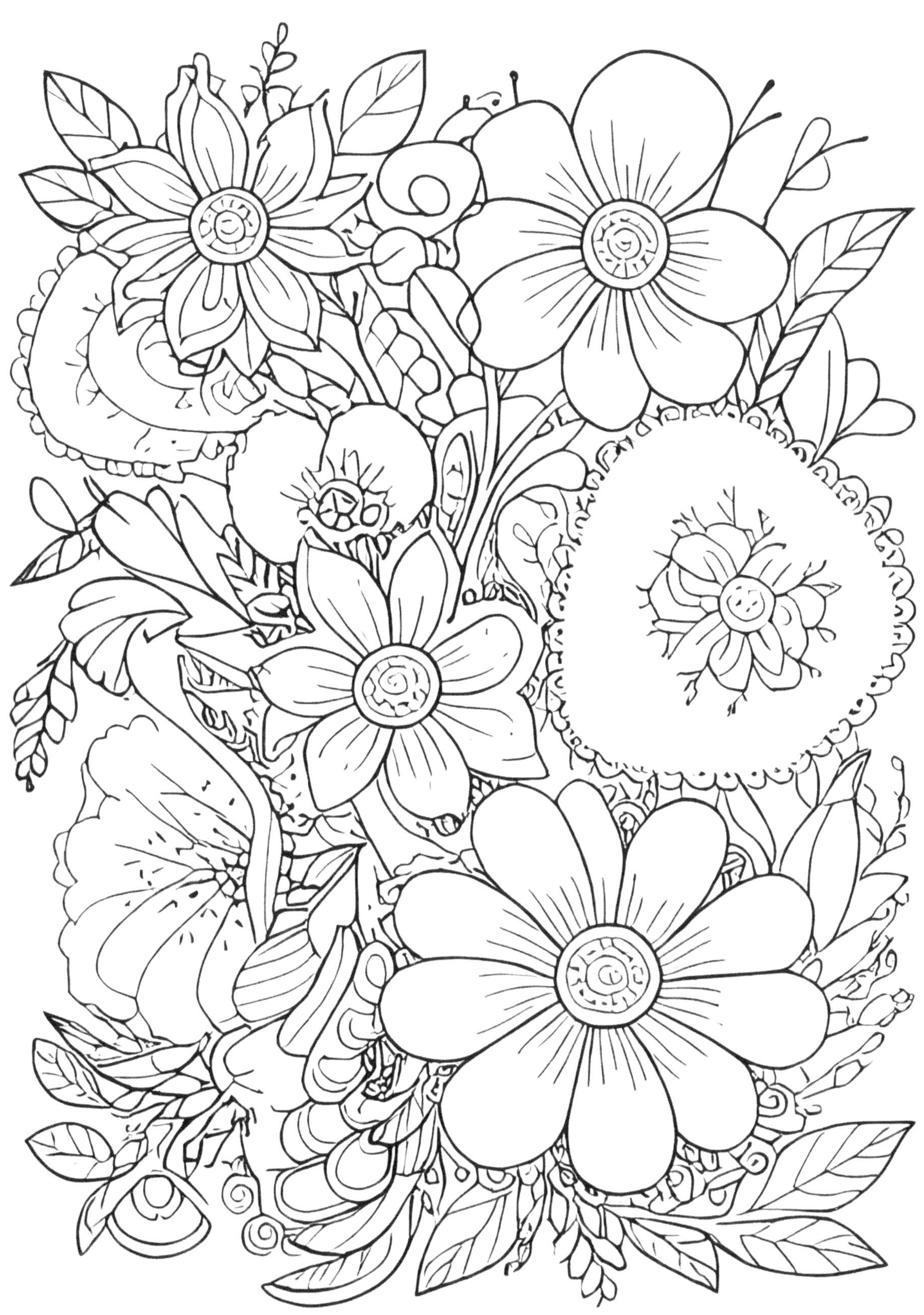

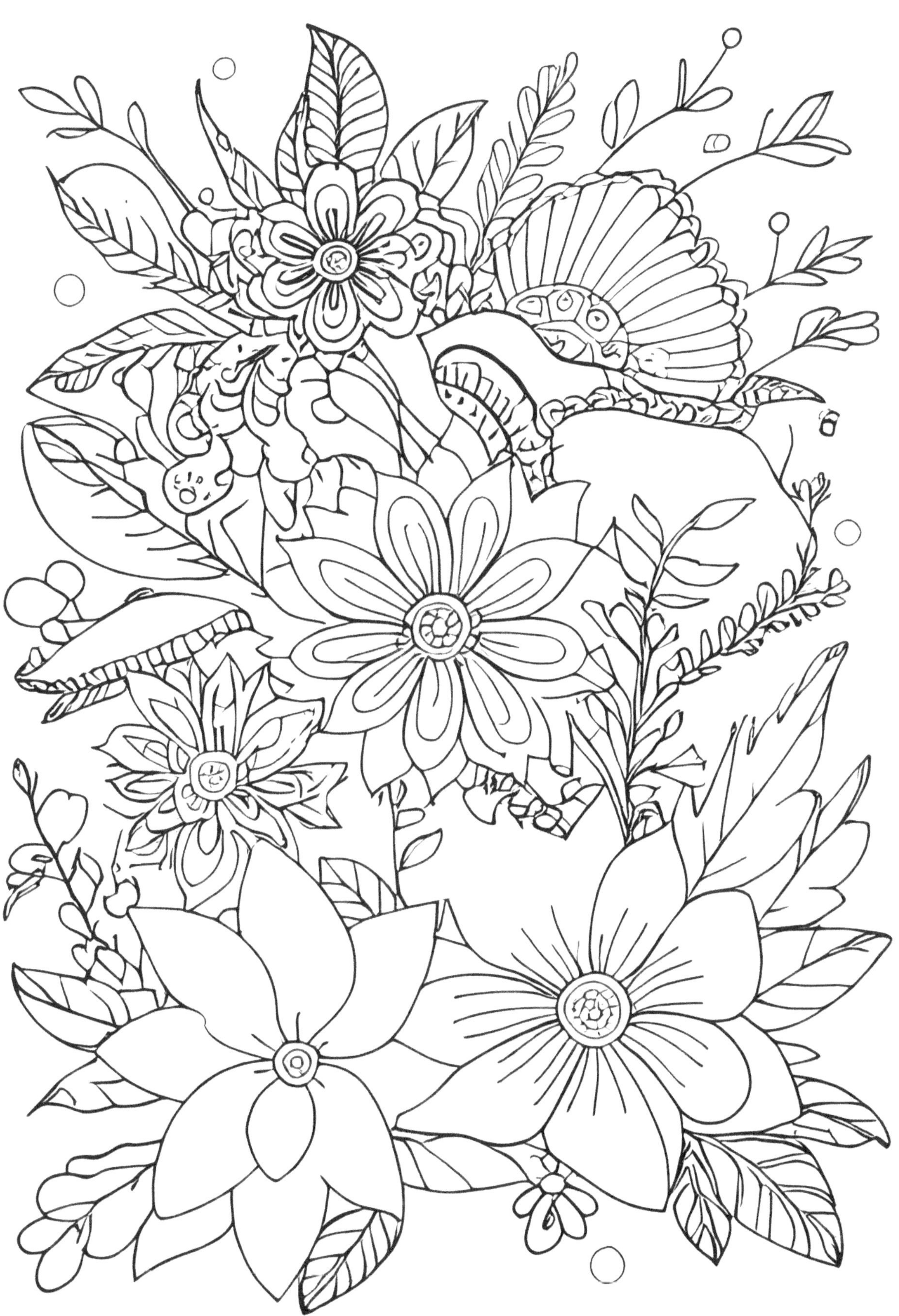

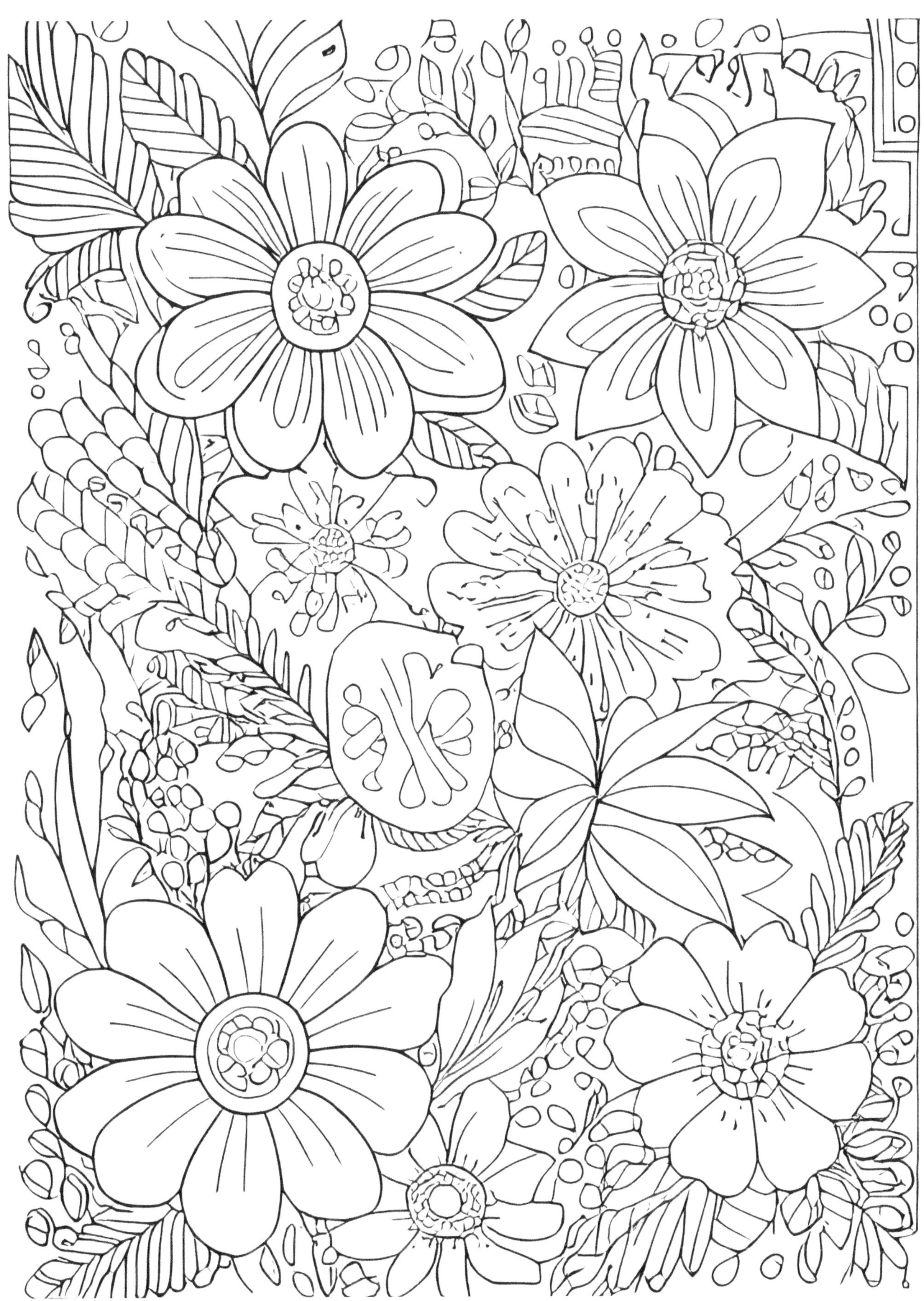

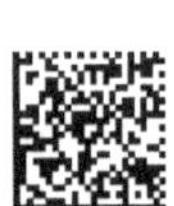